THE
LIBERTY®
HOME

THE LIBERTY® HOME

Distinctive Sewing Projects from Classic Liberty Fabrics

edited by Ljiljana Baird
illustrated by Penny Brown

CB
CONTEMPORARY BOOKS

ACKNOWLEDGMENTS

"Liberty Style, Arthur Lasenby Liberty: A Mere Adjective?" by Sarah Nichols, chief curator
and curator of decorative arts, Carnegie Museum of Art, Pittsburg, PA, reprinted from
The Journal of Decorative and Propaganda Arts, no 13 (Summer 1989): pp76–93 ©1989
The Wolfson Foundation of Decorative and Propaganda Arts, Inc.

The publisher would like to thank the following for their hard work and dedication:
Jane Walmsley for designing and making the projects for the Kitchen; Claire Terry for the designs
for the Dining Room, Living Room and Dressing Room; to Sue Whimster and her team for turning the projects
into reality; to Joy Branscombe of You Toucan Quilt, Bedminster, UK for the cot quilt; to Annlee Landman and
Ngaire Brooks. Our sincere thanks to the Liberty team for their help and co-operation in putting this book together.
Many thanks to Alison Kenney at Westminster Archives Centre, London, UK; to Jenni Dobson, Ray Daffurn,
Anny Evason and Norman Hollands.

The photographs at pages 1–7, 9–11, 16–21, 24–35, 38–39, 42–44, 46–47, 49–51, 53–57, 59, 63–65, 67, 69–78, 81,
83–87, 89, 91–97, 99–101, 103–111, 113, 118, 120–121, 123, 125, 127, 130, 132 and the jacket
© Liberty PLC 1997 and have been provided courtesy of Liberty PLC. None of these images may be reproduced or
stored in any manner or form whatsoever without the express written consent of Liberty PLC.

Liberty ® is a registered Trade Mark of Liberty PLC. Its use and inclusion in this work gives no licence or authority
for its use in any other manner or context.

Published by MQ Publications, Ltd.
254-258 Goswell Road, London EC1V 7EB, UK

Editors: Ljiljana Ortolja-Baird and Simona Hill
Design: Wilson Design Associates

Library of Congress Cataloging-in-Publication Data

The Liberty home : distinctive sewing projects from classic Liberty fabrics / edited by Ljiljana Baird.
    p. cm
Includes index.
ISBN: 0-8092-2988-9
 1. House furnishing. 2. Textile fabrics in interior decoration.
3. Liberty & Co. I Baird, Ljiljana
TT387.L53 1997
746.9--dc21   97-14820
                              CIP

Contents

The Liberty Style

ARTHUR LASENBY LIBERTY: A MERE ADJECTIVE?

In 1913, Arthur Lasenby Liberty received a knighthood in recognition of the significant role he had played in promoting the decorative arts in Britain. He was seventy years old and very much in charge of the business on Regent Street which still bears his name. The knighthood gave the press a reason to review his career, and *The Daily Chronicle* wrote an article, "The House of Liberty and Its Founder," based on an interview with Sir Arthur. Among other topics, Sir Arthur discussed the firm's success in introducing to fabrics the delicate and subtle shades which had become known all over the world as Liberty colors. He finished the interview by stating, "I am afraid that in this and other respects I have become a mere adjective."

Literature on the firm, both modern and contemporary, upholds this statement. For example, catalogs issued by the company as early as 1883 used the term Liberty Art Fabrics, and a furniture catalog of around 1910 illustrated rooms

Above: Liberty's Tudor building, Great Marlborough Street, London, UK, built by Edwin T. Hall and E. Stanley Hall was completed in 1925. The design gives the appearance of a row of several shops rather than one large store. The timbers used—oak and teak were salvaged from two old men-of-war ships the H. M. S. Impregnable and the H. M. S. Hindustan.

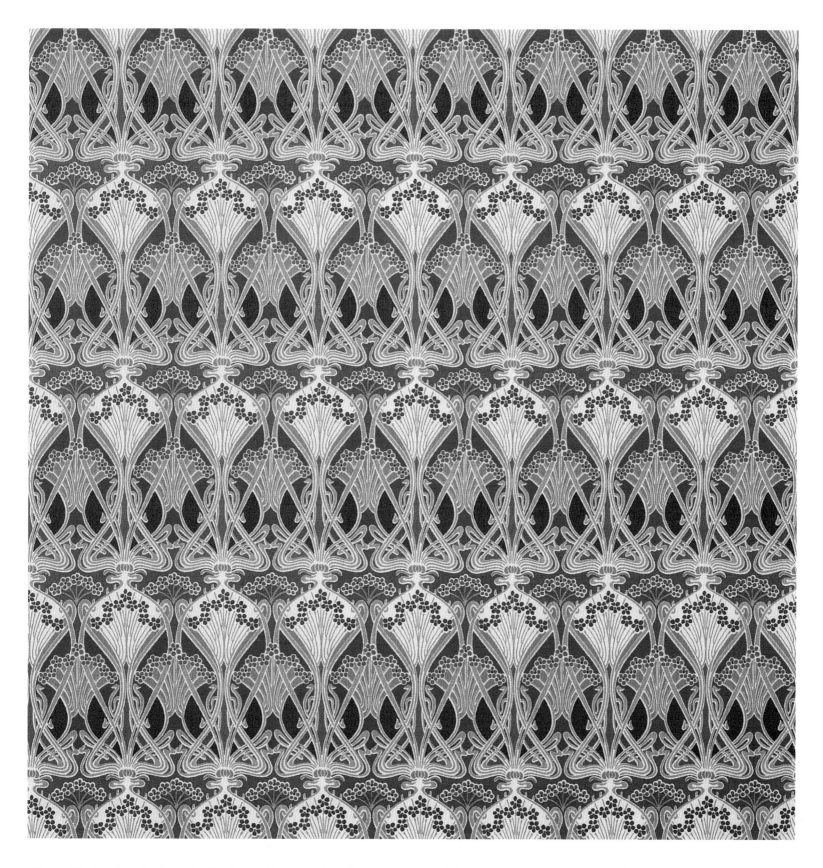

Above: The Ianthe print from the Chesham collection, universally associated with Liberty, was designed around 1900 by an unknown designer. It epitomises Liberty's particular interpretation of Art Nouveau—a blend of the sinuous interlacing line of European Art Nouveau with Celtic ornamentation and the tempering functionalism of the Arts and Crafts movement. Arthur Liberty championed the Art Nouveau movement but abhorred European developments and after viewing an exhibition of drawings and paintings in Budapest in 1909 declared: "…L'Art Nouveau has been brought into contempt by gross exaggeration."

designated as being in the Liberty style, although the name was nearly always in inverted commas. The artistic and business press of 1900, who celebrated the passing of the century and the firm's 25th birthday, were in no doubt about the significance of the store on Regent Street, its founder, and his name. According to an article in the magazine *Fortunes Made in Business: Life Struggles of Successful People*, "Libertyism, if it may be so called, is not a fad or a fashion, it is a firmly established movement, that touches the love of the artistic which is born in everyone [sic] of us, the taught and the untaught." *The Art Journal* of February 1900, in its article "The Growth of an Influence," was no less insistent on the importance of Liberty "he has built up an influence that has laid hold of almost every section of society, and has been responsible for a radical change in the general opinion on aesthetic questions. He has made a style different in many ways from anything previously existing and has cultivated it until it has gained an authority that is universally admitted." Modern authors are no less reticent about using Liberty's name as an adjective. Two recent publications, the catalog of an exhibition organised by Victor Arwas and held in Japan in 1983 and a book by Mervyn Levy published in 1986, both focusing on the period 1895 to 1910, have used Liberty Style as their titles.

What was this style, and can it be defined? Certainly, though the press of 1900 made no attempt to do so. Can it be equated with the *art nouveau* movement, as suggested by Mario Amaya in his 1963 article "Liberty and the Modern Style" and by the fact that the movement in Italy came to be known as *stile Liberty*. Was the press of 1900 correct in proposing that the business represented a movement that had "laid hold of every section of society and…created an entirely distinct standard of taste and that Liberty has revolutionized the world's opinion on aesthetic questions?" Only an examination of the whole scope of the business in the period around 1900, emphasizing the key areas of fabrics, furniture, and metalwork, and the views of Sir Arthur himself, will reveal the answers.

Liberty's was successful around 1900 because of the solid foundations laid from the moment the store commenced trading in 1875 (initially with only three employees) at 218A Regent Street, grandly renamed East India House. By this date, Liberty had already amassed twelve years' experience in the retail import business, the last ten as manager of Farmer and Roger's Oriental warehouse. He built up his department until it became the most profitable side of the business as well as an important meeting place for advocates of the aesthetic movement. When he was refused a partnership, he was ready to set up on his own, no novice but an experienced and well-connected retailer.

The vogue for Oriental wares during this period was part and parcel of the aesthetic movement. By virtue of being at the center of retailing such goods, Liberty played a central role in the establishment and popularity of the movement. He was the friend and, if you believe him, mentor of many key figures, as the statement illustrates: "Whistler always pretended that he valued my critical judgement, and certainly we had a feeling of sympathy of the Japanese impressionist side of things. I remember spending many hours with him when he was engaged on the famous peacock room, and it was a pleasant pose of his to suggest that I assisted him with advice." This may be wishful thinking on Liberty's part, although an article written by the architect, designer, and key aesthetic movement figure E. W. Godwin, describing Liberty's shop and its customers in 1876, lauds it as the meeting place of the social elite and the place to see and be seen. Liberty's shop was an overnight success, and the stock immediately expanded to cover many different types of Oriental wares, not simply fabrics. Soon Liberty was importing goods from other parts of the world as well.

The next stage in his rapid expansion program was to augment, and for fabrics eventually to substitute, the imported goods with items manufactured in Britain. This was a shrewd move for several reasons. Liberty knew that the mania for things Japanese, even if it could be sustained, would not keep up with his ever-growing ambitions. With the popularization of Japanese taste in the West, the inevitable happened; the quality of goods from Japan lessened, a fact commented on by Godwin in his 1876 article. Liberty could not hope to control and dictate to manufacturers from far-flung parts of the globe. Also realizing that Eastern and Oriental fabrics were not ideally suited to everyday English tastes and the vicissitudes of the climate, he started looking for English manufacturers and designers to provide his stock, initially using imported plain silks or unwoven

Below: *Page from catalog ca. 1900 advertising perennial favorites in Oriental wares.*

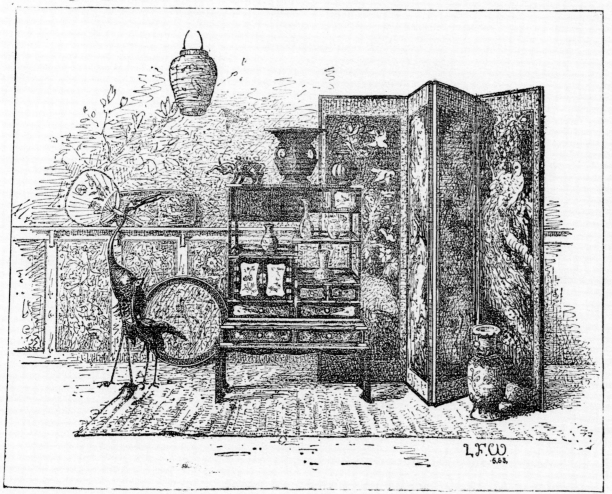

❈ Japanese ◆ Furniture ◆ and ◆ Decoration. ❈

Four-fold Handsome Satin Screens, embroidered,
90/-
With Gold in rich designs of Birds and Flowers,
From 10 Guineas.
Paper ditto from 30/-

Lacquer and Enamel Cabinets, fitted with Drawers and Shelves, delicate and beautiful work,
From 5 to 100 Guineas.

Lacquer Trays in all sizes and qualities,
From 9d. each.

Hand Screens of all kinds,
From 2d. each.

Bronze Storks, finely cast and finished.

Paper Lanterns in various colours,
From 1/- to 5/-

Bronze Griffin, very curious and quaint.

Bronze Vases and Ornaments,
From 50/-

Jars in Porcelain of every native make and design.

Fine Grass Matting, one yard wide,
2s. per yard.

Leather Paper for Wall Decoration,
2/- and 2/6 per yard.

wool. For example, Nagpore silk made in India was shipped raw to England and dyed by a permanent process especially for Liberty. Umritza cashmere, developed by Liberty from 1879, was made of pure Indian wool imported and woven in England to combine softness of touch with durability and a price much lower than the native Indian handwoven cashmeres. Liberty fabrics were intended for clothes and light furnishings. To capitalize on their potential uses, Liberty set up an upholstery department in 1882 and, in the following year, a furniture and design department. He did not trust others to make up his gracefully draping materials correctly, so he founded a costume department in 1884. Business was expanding, but it was not an unnatural progression. Liberty's entrepreneurial flair was sowing seeds for growth not dependent on Japonisme or an import warehouse but on fabrics, and British-produced fabrics at that.

Liberty Art Fabrics were so well established by 1887 that other manufacturers and retailers "as destitute of originality and commercial honesty" were pirating and copying them. In that year, the firm made an application against another London store, The Army and Navy, to restrain it from selling fabrics manufactured under the Liberty banner. It is rather hard to be sure from extant records what constituted Liberty Art Fabrics in the 1880s. Surviving catalogs of this time contain small swatches, primarily of plain or small Indian print design, implying that the variety of colors and the character of the material itself are the important factors. An advertisement from the late 1880s has nubile young ladies scantily clad in artistically draped flowing material, thus stressing the inherent quality of Liberty fabrics to hang beautifully. Press extracts in the 1887 catalog praising the fabrics, particularly the Umritza cashmere, concentrate on their softness, suppleness, serviceability, quality, price, color range, and gracefulness of draping; no mention is made of the design of the fabrics. Yet in the same year, the famous peacock feather fabric [see page 127] designed by Arthur Silver and manufactured for Liberty's by the Rossendale Printing Company was shown at the Manchester Royal Jubilee

Exhibition. This design has become synonymous with the Liberty name, but the catalog gives no hint of the important role these arts and crafts movement fabrics were to play in the firm's growth.

Dramatic changes were taking place in the textile industry in the fourth quarter of the nineteenth century, and Liberty's was just one component of the volatile scene. New manufacturers, new designers, new and revived materials and production processes, and new retailing and consumption patterns all contributed to the upheaval. These various elements meant that working relationships between manufacturers, designers and retailers were complex and hard to unravel. There were no set rules as to who initiated and who controlled, although Liberty was in no doubt that he was in charge at all times and trained manufacturers up to his standards. However, he was not the only force at work. Other businessmen such as Thomas Wardle—a textile dyer and printer from Leek in Staffordshire and, like Liberty, an active advocate of the revival of the silk industry in England—played important roles. The designers also found a voice in this period through the Arts

Below: An advertisement for Liberty Art Fabrics, late 1880s.

Left: Arthur Silver for Liberty & Co., printed cotton design, ca.1896. Photograph courtesy of Nordenfjelske Kunstindustrimuseum, Trondheim, Norway.

and Crafts Exhibition Society. Founded in 1887, they held their first exhibition the following year and continued to mount exhibitions on an intermittent basis until 1916. The society not only gave its name to the arts and crafts movement in Britain but also provided a forum for discussion and a focal point for the promotion of new designs. Textile design at that time can only be defined in extremely broad terms because it encompassed such a vast range, particularly from 1893 to 1903—the most innovative, diverse and significant period for fabrics of the arts and crafts movement. This broad spectrum was represented on the one hand by the flat, geometric, solid color-block designs of Lindsay Butterfield or C. F. A. Voysey and on the other by the fluid, swirling patterns of the Silver Studio. Although stylistically varied, the one overriding theme of textiles of this period was the use of botanical motifs, inspired by a resurgence of interest in gardening and garden design. It is surprisingly hard to pinpoint exactly which fabrics were or were not retailed through Liberty's, and as a consequence, what, if anything, differentiated the firm from other leading and fashionable retailers such as Heal's. Existing evidence certainly shows that the complete sphere of modern design was available through Liberty's.

Textiles were easily transportable, and so a ready-made vehicle for the transference of style, ideas and the Liberty name from Britain to the Continent. Sales were promoted and facilitated by the Paris branch and augmented by agents throughout Europe. Liberty fabrics were available and popular in many countries. For example, in deference to the graceful draping quality of Liberty silks, in France the term "*soie Liberty*" was used for any softly draping silk. In the 1890s, Erik Folcher ran a shop specializing in the wares of the English arts and crafts movement in Stockholm, Sweden. He had about 2000 textile samples to show his clients, of which more than 1700 were from Liberty's, giving some indication of the firm's dominance of the marketplace. At that time, Liberty fabrics were also acquired for museum collections. For example, in 1896 and 1897 the Kunstindustrimuseum in Trondheim, Norway, purchased several examples in Paris either directly from Liberty's or from Siegfried Bing's shop, thus documenting at least a minute proportion of the designs retailed by the firm. Liberty claimed that his fabrics led the field in the 1880s as far as quality and character of material went, but by 1900, the designs he sold represented the complete spectrum of modern British textile design, marketed under the Liberty banner.

Throughout history, textiles have played an important role in interior decoration. The late nineteenth century was no exception, and Liberty fabrics were used in interiors as well as for clothes. To capture this potential and profitable market, Liberty set up an upholstery studio in 1882. The furnishing and decorating studio was founded in the following year to bring everything together in a unified way to "ensure the success of the ensemble." As far as upholstery was concerned, the concept of a Liberty style certainly existed by 1894, the date of a telling cartoon in *Punch*, and it clearly represented good taste, however defined. "We're very proud of this room, Mrs. Homing. Our own little upholsterer did it up just as you see it, and all our friends think it was *Liberty*!" says the hostess about her over-upholstered chair. The firm did nothing to dispel the idea of a Liberty style, or at least the use of the name as an adjective, and two of its marketing and design policies actively promoted and fostered the concept. First, all the designs were marketed anonymously. Designers' names were never given. This ruling applied equally to in-house designs and those commissioned from outside or brought in from manufacturers. Occasionally a designer's name might be attached to a Liberty object published in *The Studio*, and the entries submitted by Liberty's to the Arts and Crafts Exhibition Society exhibitions were required to include the name of the designer, but these were exceptions that proved the Liberty rule. Other manufacturers and retailers were less strict about maintaining the anonymity of their designers, particularly when they had made a name for themselves in other fields, such as the architect Voysey. Liberty's however, adhered religiously to its rule, only naming designers as a last resort. Second, no design submitted to Liberty's was sacred. Drawings from outside designers were altered by the in-house studio to suit the firm's requirements. An Archibald Knox pewter candlestick is a prime example of this mix-and-match mentality. Knox's original design had two cups, one on each side of the single stick. This candlestick did appear with minor modifications, such as a plain base or one inset with stones, but it was also produced with a third central cup, a rather unsuccessful Liberty adaptation. Tampering with designs was clearly not unusual. In 1913, Denise Tuckfield, a student of Knox's who worked for Liberty's, reported back to him that she saw members of the design staff "tracing the body of one design, combining this with the handle from another and the spout from still a third design." Hardly surprisingly, echoes of many of the leading designers of the day are frequently found in Liberty's products.

With the foundation of the furnishing and decorating studio, the next major area Liberty launched himself into was furniture. In 1900, he gave a lecture to the Society of Arts. Although primarily an outline of the history of furniture before 1800, with very little comment on the contemporary, this lecture provides a good insight into Liberty's philosophy about furniture's form, decoration, and purpose. Many of his abstract ideas carry over into other media. Liberty believed furniture was not made to be looked at but to be used: "Better a Windsor chair with comfort than a chaise à la Louis Quinze which makes one's back ache…Utility which means fitness is in itself beauty if rightly understood." However, Liberty did allow that furniture could be decorated provided that the decoration was controlled: "Inlay of all kinds ought to be strictly kept within bounds. Like carving it is a good servant but a bad master, good marquetry never attempts to suggest a picture." Liberty was very scathing about the "unspeakable rococo," although he did approve of the ormolu workers of the Louis XV period. He clearly liked the use of metalwork on furniture provided it fulfilled the three criteria he laid down: having a distinct purpose which could not be fulfilled by wood alone, showing its purpose plainly, and being good in itself. Good outline and good proportion were essential to produce excellence in form and sound construction: "The curved line is only admissible as an adjunct to these and should always be subordinate." He did not comment on modern furniture, but no doubt would have wholeheartedly agreed with the review in *The Studio* of Hector Guimard's furniture shown at the Salon du Champs du Mars in 1897, classing it as an example of the worst possible taste, fit only for cannibals. This was not an isolated view. The consensus of British opinion was on Liberty's side; furniture should be vertical and horizontal rather than curved, and not overly decorated. In

Right: Arthur Silver for Liberty & Co., printed cotton design, ca. 1896. Photograph courtesy of Nordenfjelske Kunstindustrimuseum, Trondheim, Norway.

Left: *"Nerrisa" gown and Art Nouveau furnishings from Liberty's Dress and Decoration catalog, ca. 1905. English, early 18th century dress and tea jacket robe of soft silk. Jacket of velveteen with gauze front. Collar and cuffs embroidered design in appliqué.*

Right and below: The Moorish room from
The Liberty Handbook of Sketches, ca.
1890–95. Although not as far reaching in
popularity as Japanese style interiors, Liberty's
did supply clients with designs and furnishings
for Moorish smoking rooms, Arab halls and
Moorish music rooms. Clients for the Arab
vogue included Frederick Leighton whose house
in Holland Park Road, London, is preserved as
a museum and the Marquess of Aberdeen
whose house was also graced by the artists,
aesthetes and dilettantes of the period.

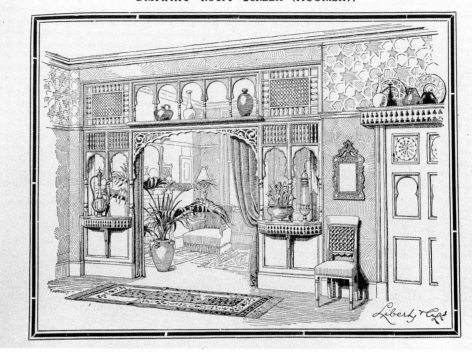

DRAWING · ROOM · SCREEN (MOORISH).

DRAWING · ROOM · SCREEN (MOORISH).

 design is here
shewn for a type
of screen suitable
for placing across
Bay Windows,
dividing the rooms,
etc. Numerous
examples in other
styles may be
noted in some of the preceding
illustrations. ●●●●●●●●●●●

Messrs. LIBERTY have a large
number of sketches in their folios of
screens and arches suitable for every
position, a selection of which they
will be pleased to forward; and on
receipt of particulars and sizes, they
will be pleased to quote an exact
price and, if necessary, to forward
a special drawing to suit the character
of the room. ●●●●●●●●●●●●●

general, the furniture retailed by Liberty, whether in the arts and crafts framework
or straight reproduction, followed his ideas on form, decoration, and fitness for use.

One of Liberty's most famous furniture designs was the Thebes stool, based on
an Egyptian form, which was available in a three- and a four-legged version.
Designed in 1884, it was made until 1907 and illustrates another characteristic of
Liberty's furniture designs, longevity. The Thebes stool was sold extensively
throughout Europe and stocked by Bing in his Paris shop. Although the three-
legged version with its curved legs appealed to art nouveau taste, it really owed its
success to the same interest in the exotic and Oriental that popularized Moorish
octagonal tables and chairs with Arab fretwork backs, both of which were available
through Liberty's. The origins of the business as an Oriental warehouse had not
been totally abandoned.

Philosophically, Liberty was a great advocate of the machine, but stylistically, the firm produced furniture in the arts and crafts tradition. It was angular and frequently had projecting cornices or extended vertical elements, motifs that echoed earlier designs of the Century Guild and Voysey. At the top of the market, the furniture was made of mahogany and strikingly inlaid, not only with lighter woods but sometimes mother-of-pearl and abalone shell as well, creating a richer

Right and below: The Culloden dining room from The Liberty Handbook of Sketches, ca. 1890–95. This sideboard in a slightly modified form was still being produced by the firm nearly twenty years later.

"CULLODEN" · DINING · ROOM (GERMAN GOTHIC).

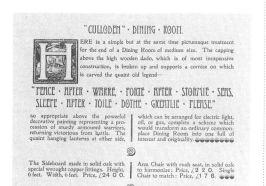

"CULLODEN" · DINING · ROOM.

HERE is a simple but at the same time picturesque treatment for the end of a Dining Room of medium size. The capping above the high wooden dado, which is of most inexpensive construction, is broken up and supports a cornice on which is carved the quaint old legend—

"PEACE · AFTER · WARRE, · PORTE · AFTER · STORMIE · SEAS, SLEEPE · AFTER · TOILE · DOTHE · GREATLIE · PLEASE."

so appropriate above the powerful decorative painting representing a procession of sturdy armoured warriors, returning victorious from battle. The quaint hanging lanterns at either side, which can be arranged for electric light, oil, or gas, complete a scheme which would transform an ordinary commonplace Dining Room into one full of interest and originality.

The Sideboard made in solid oak with special wrought copper fittings. Height, 6 feet. Width, 6 feet. Price, £24 0 0. Arm Chair with rush seat, in solid oak to harmonize: Price, £2 2 0. Single Chair to match: Price, £1 7 6.

and more varied surface than the plain, rather austere oak furniture Liberty's also sold. The oak furniture harked back to pre-industrial medieval and Renaissance sources, reflecting Liberty's belief that the accession of James I marked the beginning of the finest period of British taste. It is occasionally hard to tell where a modern arts and crafts interpretation leaves off and a reproduction style takes over, particularly in the sideboard designs. Unadulterated reproduction furniture completed the range retailed by Liberty's.

As well as providing furniture in a multiplicity of styles, Liberty's could also supply appropriate interiors. Two catalogs in the Liberty Archive at Westminster City Libraries show furniture in room settings. Neither catalog is dated, but the earlier one, *The Liberty Handbook of Sketches*, probably dates from 1890 to 1895 and the later one, *Furniture by Liberty & Co.*, from around 1905 to 1910. The differences and similarities between the two catalogs are telling. Both illustrate several of the same sideboard designs, with only minor alterations, though possibly twenty years had elapsed. In the earlier catalog, several interiors are labelled "recent developments and adaptations." The texts accompanying these illustrations are descriptive and do not elucidate the aesthetics of recent developments or enumerate the changes. However, they percolate with arts and crafts overtones,

HOUSE DECORATION

Liberty Colour and Liberty Design, as applied to Dress and Furnishing Fabrics, are well known.

To follow " the craze of the moment," when decorating and furnishing the home, is to court disappointment.

Liberty & Co.'s knowledge of colour and design, as applied to House Decoration and Furniture, enables them to produce a dignified, as well as a distinctive, result in the treatment of any room.

These qualities combined with sound materials and good craftsmanship give lasting pleasure and satisfaction.

During the present trade depression and with the idea of keeping their joiners and workmen employed, Liberty & Co. are willing to prepare (free of cost) estimates for

ENGLISH OAK FITMENTS & PANELLING of the same quality and workmanship (with Carving, if desired) as in

THEIR OWN TUDOR BUILDING

at **10% on cost**

LIBERTY & Co., Ltd., Regent St., LONDON

Left: Liberty's advertisement for interior decorating services. 1931. The services of the Contracts Department were kept busy with private as well as public commissions.

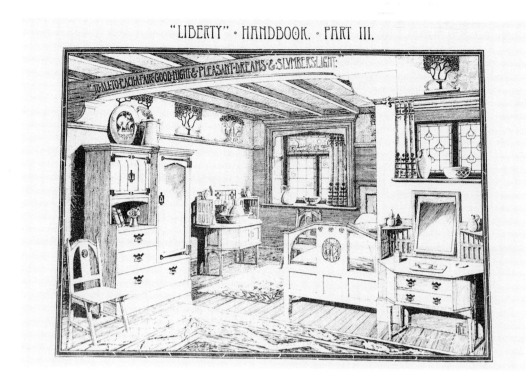

"LIBERTY" · HANDBOOK. · PART III.

Left: *"To All To Each A Fair Good Night of Pleasant Dreams and Slumbers Light."* *Bedroom design from the Liberty Handbook of Sketches, ca. 1890–95.*

Right: *Verso page of Bedroom design from the Liberty Handbook of Sketches, ca. 1890–95.*

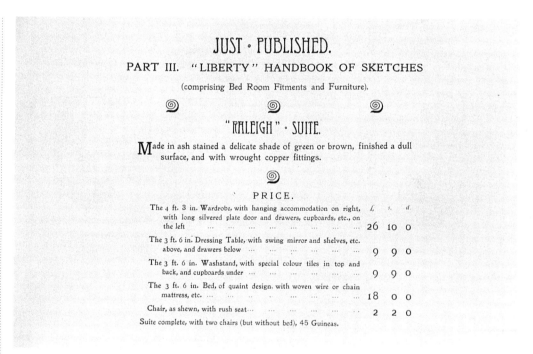

JUST · PUBLISHED.

PART III. "LIBERTY" HANDBOOK OF SKETCHES

(comprising Bed Room Fitments and Furniture).

"RALEIGH" · SUITE.

Made in ash stained a delicate shade of green or brown, finished a dull surface, and with wrought copper fittings.

PRICE.

	£	s.	d.
The 4 ft. 3 in. Wardrobe, with hanging accommodation on right, with long silvered plate door and drawers, cupboards, etc., on the left	26	10	0
The 3 ft. 6 in. Dressing Table, with swing mirror and shelves, etc. above, and drawers below	9	9	0
The 3 ft. 6 in. Washstand, with special colour tiles in top and back, and cupboards under	9	9	0
The 3 ft. 6 in. Bed, of quaint design, with woven wire or chain mattress, etc.	18	0	0
Chair, as shewn, with rush seat	2	2	0

Suite complete, with two chairs (but without bed), 45 Guineas.

focusing on construction points and fitness for use, and the sketches give a sense of the Liberty style coming together in an interior. A good example is the bedroom with its suitable motto, standard motifs (such as a ship in full sail and trees and birds) recurring in different guises, and plain oak arts and crafts furniture with decorative and structural elements repeated in different pieces. The same unity and strong sense of style, as well as an emphasis on fabrics is seen in a bedroom designed by Liberty's and displayed in the Regent Street shop in 1897. The early twentieth century catalog titles certain interiors as being in the Liberty style, but these, appear rather lack lustre by comparison to previous interiors. The cutting edge seems to have gone. Judging from this catalog, the balance between

the arts and craft and reproduction styles shifts, and the reproduction side takes command. As this later catalog states, "To realise how beautiful a modern reproduction can be, you must go to Liberty's." Even the arts and crafts models, based on designs of possibly twenty years earlier which seemed fresh and new then, were lacking in sparkle by 1910.

The next stage in the expansion program after interiors and furniture was metalware. Liberty had been selling silver and pewter from various sources for some time before he considered organizing its production himself. In 1899, a small exhibition of wares specifically commissioned by Liberty and made in London was held at the Regent Street shop. This was the start of the new Cymric silver line. In 1900, Liberty introduced a pewter line marketed as Tudric. These two established and popularized the Celtic revival style in Britain.

In 1904, Liberty delivered another lecture to the Society of Arts. The topic this time was "Pewter and the Revival of its Use." The presentation was rather technical and historically based, but odd glimpses of Liberty's ideas on style and workmanship emerged. Liberty proposed that he alone was behind the revival of the pewter industry in Britain and the revival of the Celtic style. He did not mention Archibald Knox, the most interesting and innovative of his metalwork designers and one of the key proponents of the Celtic revival style.

Born and bred in the Isle of Man, a Celtic haven, Knox also went to art school there and expressed his heritage by choosing to make a special study of Celtic design for his final exam in historical ornament. Knox was not the only designer in this period fascinated by interlaced Celtic strapwork. Owen Jones published three plates of Celtic ornament in *The Grammar of Ornament* in 1856, and L. C. Tiffany used Celtic knots to decorate a covered silver beaker in 1878.

Many of the pieces designed by Knox are decorated with Celtic strapwork, from one simple strand to highly complex interlaced patterns impossible to unravel. Not satisfied with strapwork being merely ornamental, he also used it as part of the structural configuration of objects. However, Knox was not simply a regurgitator of Celtic motifs, having too much integrity and vision to be a mere copyist, as attested by his metalwork designs. He produced extremely innovative shapes reminiscent of bullets or rockets, anticipating the streamlining of the machine age by thirty years. He used enamel as decoration, and Liberty's craftsmen were able to produce blue-greens of unbelievable richness that have hardly been paralleled since, enhancing the metal surface with both color and texture. The semi-precious stones he frequently advocated using produced the same effect. In keeping with the arts and crafts spirit, a number of his pieces, particularly the clocks, contain a thought-provoking motto. Knox produced fabric/wallpaper designs [see photograph left] as well as ones for metalware. They were based on botanical motifs, like most fabrics of the day, but managed to combine a high degree of abstraction—much more than that achieved by Voysey or Butterfield—with great flow and movement. Needless to say, they were so far from the mainstream that they were never produced in Knox's lifetime. It would be interesting to know if he ever submitted them to Liberty's, and if so, what their reaction was.

Like many people from humble backgrounds who make good, Liberty became a pillar of the community, combining civic duty with continued hard work in business. Following his move to the country estate of Lee Manor, Buckingham-shire, Liberty led a conventional country squire's life. His personal taste, judging admittedly from only one photograph of the drawing room at Lee Manor, appears rather conservative. Although there is a Thebes stool in the foreground and a hint of whimsy in the bronze stork, the furniture is extremely traditional. On the piano there is an over-upholstered lamp, reminiscent of the interior in the 1894 *Punch* cartoon. Perhaps the rather pointed aside in the cartoon would have fallen flat if the truth as to his personal tastes were known. But clearly, Liberty's own taste is not the way to define the style. It is the business that bears his name that has become the adjective, not the man.

Even in key areas like fabric, metalwork, and furniture, pinpointing the Liberty style is difficult. In the 1880s, the name "Liberty" attached to fabric denoted quality and color range. By 1900, Liberty sold the best in British design and manufacture. But the stylistic diversity of the fabrics of the arts and crafts movement and the complex interrelationships of the many significant designers and manufacturers mean that an all-embracing definition is impossible to come by. Metalwork presents a much more cohesive picture, especially if one concentrates on the designs of Archibald Knox. The firm was clearly directing both design and manufacture and making a strong stylistic statement due to the brilliance and single-mindedness of Knox. However, his work was not the whole picture. A 1910 catalog from Liberty's Manchester branch illustrated pewter objects copying eighteenth-century silver designs as well as contemporary shapes decorated with Celtic strapwork. The traditional and the modern co-existed. Furniture and interiors present the least cohesive view of a Liberty style. The arts and crafts movement, the reproduction styles, and the middle-class concern for surface richness and decoration existed in conflict rather than harmony until 1900, when reproduction styles appear to have won. Furniture and interiors were not as easily transportable as fabrics and metalware, so Europe was spared some of this confusion. A Liberty style, visually speaking, only exists if one is rather selective and uses a broad brush to define it. Such a definition does not do justice to the comprehensive nature of the business and Liberty's achievement, for by the early years of the twentieth century, everything for the modern home, from electrical generators through wooden paneling and plasterwork ceilings to cushions and thimbles, could be purchased from Liberty's.

The best representation of this selective Liberty style is provided by the firm itself in a dress and decoration catalog from around 1905 which contains beautiful colored plates of elegant ladies languishing in interior settings. Furniture, fabrics, and even metalwork come together. The brief introductory text by Arthur Fish mentions the role Liberty played in "the emancipation from slavish subjection to passing fashion." Fish was referring specifically to dress, but the notion can be expanded to include all aspects of interior decoration. This emancipation meant that Liberty's could offer artistic choice, which perhaps explains the wide range of styles available in all the products retailed by the firm. However, Fish sounded a note of caution, for artistic freedom was a dangerous commodity: "Individuality can formulate general ideas and taste can control them within the right bounds but there is needed the deeper knowledge that can only be acquired by the specialist to ensure the success of the ensemble." That specialist was obviously

Above: The "Henrietta" Charles II house gown and interior. A flowered Tyrian silk skirt with high-waisted bodice of velveteen and fichu with sleeves in silk crêpe. From the Liberty Dress and Decoration catalog, ca. 1905.

Right: *"Amelia" Empire evening gown with coat and furnishings. The robe of Orion satin is embroidered in harmonious coloring. The coat of silk-velvet is lined with satin; collar, cuffs and belt embroidered with silk and appliqué velvet. From Liberty's Dress and Decoration catalog, ca 1905.*

Liberty. He encouraged his customers to look afresh at their domestic surroundings and "to gratify in their own homes the love of color of the beatific in form and fabric which is inherent in us all," whether in the Jacobean, Louis XVI, arts and crafts, or Liberty style. If such a thing as the Liberty style exists, and the name is used as an adjective, the key to understanding its meaning is not through selected individual objects retailed by the firm but through Liberty's own vision of the role of his store in educating consumers and manufacturers alike by imposing certain standards across a wide range of goods, services, and styles.

Getting Started

When designing the furnishing and decorations for a room, a pinboard will provide an invaluable visual reminder of all the elements that you want to include in your scheme. For each of the rooms I have assembled my own pinboards, with the various inspirations that have helped formulate the final design. Most of the drawings have been translated into projects—others remain as ideas only. If there are illustrated projects on the pinboards for which there are no instructions, you should have no difficulty in finding a suitable method of construction. For instance, in the dining room there are drawings for three chair covers but instructions for only one. The instructions can be adapted to make the other two chairs and to suit your own chair.

Before embarking on any significant decorating project I suggest that you prepare a pinboard of wallpaper, fabric, trimmings and paint swatches, photographs and magazine cuttings. As well as being a fun process in its own right, it acts as a screening device. Visual representations of your ideas placed side by side, often look physically different to the imagined look. The pinboard acts as a device to bring your ideas together, and then to eliminate those which don't quite work. It will help focus your attention on the focal point of the room be it an ornament, fireplace, window treatment or piece of furniture. It is also much faster and economical to discard fabric swatches and magazine cuttings, and to replace them with more suitable substitutes than it is to replace newly hung drapes and matching loose covers.

The time it takes to gather all the bits and pieces for your board also gives you more time to consider your aspirations with your actual needs. That is not to say that spontaneous decisions are incorrect, quite the contrary, often, the immediate heartfelt response is to be welcomed if after days of searching through swatch books for a suitable drape fabric you are still undecided. Also, unless the impulse purchase is so unmatchably unique you can always try to organize the rest of your room around it. This may take longer than if you had started from an overall vision. Beware though of filling your rooms with expensive impulse buys which clash and prove to be an expensive mistake. Take swatches of all your colors and fabrics with you to ensure they match. Often the shade of fabric you remember purchasing several months ago isn't quite the same as the actual version. Pinboards provide the opportunity to consider the whole room—paint, wallpaper, carpeting and fabric, not just separate aspects of it and the chance to create a scheme which works harmoniously and which you can live with happily for several years. The more time you have for preparation, the more successful your decorating projects will be.

As a precaution, when purchasing fabrics for the projects, decide first if you intend to work in imperial or metric. Buy the correct quantity stated and always work with your chosen measurement type.

Left: *Border stripe fabric from the Vittoria collection in the rust and dark green colorway.*

Projects

Kitchen

*T*he Tree of Life motif, the source of inspiration for the fabric range used in the Kitchen is well-known in the East. It came to the West with the arrival of exotic fabrics, silks, Indian chintzes, palampores and other luxurious textiles. Because of the volume of fabric arriving from India with the Tree of Life motif it was assumed that the design was Indian. Infact the flowering-tree appears earlier in Persian paintings and it is now believed that European traders instructed Indian chintz printers to supply them with patterns of "branched hangings."

The earliest Tree of Life design consists of a tree growing out of a rocky outcrop often with exposed spreading roots and bearing an abundance of fruits, flowers, foliage and often exotic birds, animals and butterflies.

The design became so popular that it was adopted by other needlework disciplines.

~ Pinboard for the Kitchen ~

The pinboard displays all the various ideas and inspirations, as well as the fabric swatches used in designing the projects for the kitchen.

I have a garden plot,
Wherin there wants nor hearbs, nor roots, nor flowers.
Flowers to smell, roots to eate, hearbs for the pot,
And dainty shelters when the welkin lowers;
Sweet smelling beds of lilies, and of roses,
Which rosemary backs and lavender encloses.
Richard Barnfield, from *The Affectionate Shepherd*, 1594

The main design motif for the kitchen is an Elizabethan knot garden. This formal design allows for an interesting mix of patchwork and appliqué when translated into fabric. The fabrics chosen for the projects are all from the Liberty's *Tree of Life* collection in the blue with yellow colorway with additional support of cobalt blue and daffodil yellow to offset the busy floral prints. I have limited the color scheme to just two colors against white, hoping to capture that astringent quality of a knot garden filled with herbs and spring bulbs.

....

1 Panel print

2 Stripe border design

3 Co-ordinating floral print

4 All-over berry design

5 All-over floral print

6 Elizabethan knot garden

7 Spring flowers—daffodils, hyacinths, crocus, lilies

8 Broderie perse appliqué

9 Carolina Lily patchwork design

10 Tapestry

Knot Garden Tablecloth

Finished size 54 x 54in/
137 x 137cm

MATERIALS

- Blue cotton ~ 1⅔yd/1.5m
- Large flower print for the border ~ 1⅛yd/1m
- Yellow cotton ~ 1yd/80cm
- Floral border print ~ 1⅔yd/ 1.5m
- White cotton ~ ⅔yd/60cm
- Berry print ~ 1⅔yd/1.5m
- Small floral print for backing ~ 3⅛yd/3m
- Low loft batting ~ 1⅔yd/1.5m
- One packet fusible webbing
- One packet tearaway stabilizer
- White sewing cotton

CUTTING

1 From blue, for the binding cut four strips 2½ x 58in/6.4 x 147.3cm along the length of the fabric. Use template E to cut four shapes and four reversed. Cut the same using template F and template I. Cut eight shapes from each of templates G and H.

2 From the large flower print, for the outer border, cut eight strips 4½ x 29in/11.4 x 73.7cm along the length of the fabric. Stitch into pairs, matching the pattern at the short end. Press the seams open.

3 From yellow, for the middle border, cut eight strips 2 x 29in/5 x 73.7cm along the length of the fabric. Join as in

Above: *Use this plan of the tablecloth as your guide to stitching the units together. The tablecloth is pieced together in four separate triangular sections which are stitched together to make the internal cross shape. The four corner squares are then added to make a square.*

step 2. Cut four shapes using template C. On the 45° bias, for the stems on the appliqué perse panels, cut eight strips 1 x 8in/2.5 x 20.3cm and eight strips 1 x 12in/2.5 x 30.5cm.

4 From the floral border print, use template A to cut four triangles from

identical positions. Cut out 48 floral motifs leaving a ¼in/6mm border around each.

5 From white, cut four shapes using template B. Cut four shapes using template J and four reversed. Mark the position of the stems.

6 From the berry fabric, for the inner border, cut four strips 2½ x 56in/ 6.4 x 142.2cm. Cut four shapes from template D and four from K. Cut four squares 7 x 7in/17.8 x 17.8cm for shape L.

7 For the backing, cut the 3⅛yd/3m length in half to yield two lengths each 58½in/1.5m. From one of these lengths cut two strips each 9in/22.9cm wide x the length of the fabric. Discard the remainder.

SEWING

• Use a ½in/1.3cm seam throughout.

1 Appliqué each of the 48 motifs in position following the instructions on page 134. Stitch three to each fabric shape B and five to each shape J.

2 To make the stems on each shape J, fold each yellow strip in half wrong sides together.

3 Leave ½in/1.3cm free at one end and pin the strip ⅛in/3mm from the folded edge to the bottom stem line. Stitch along the lower stem line.

4 Trim the raw edges of the strip almost to the stitching line.

5 Roll the folded edge over the trimmed edge and hem stitch in place. Tidy the ends. *(see pic at top of col 2)*

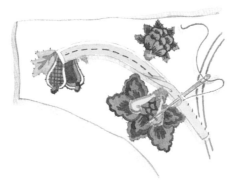

6 To make the tablecloth center, pin shape B to shape C, matching all notches first at the base of the curve, then center points. Pin at right angles to the stitching line. Stitch together. Press seams toward shape C.

7 Stitch the long straight edge of triangle A to shapes B and C.

8 Pin shape C to D in the same way. Stitch around the curve only. Remove the pins and realign the fabric to match each end of the straight seams. Pin, then stitch in place. Press the seams toward C.

9 Arrange shapes E, F, G, H and I around shape J. Clip the curved edge of J. Stitch E to J, matching notches. Stitch the long edges of the four remaining shapes to J. Press the seams away from J.

10 Stitch the diagonal seams of E and F, then E and G, G and H, and H and I together, without catching J in the stitching. Press the seams open. Repeat stitching the reverse shapes together.

11 Stitch the framed J unit to K then to the framed J reversed unit. Press seams away from K.

12 Clip the curved edge of J, K, J. Stitch to sections A–D as in step 6.

13 Stitch two panels together, matching all seams and without distorting or stretching the edges.

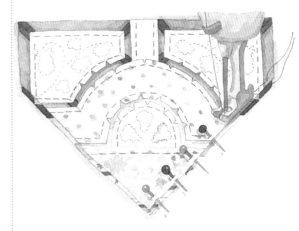

14 Stitch the two halves together, matching seams and stitching in each direction from the center outward. Press the seams in one direction.

15 Stitch the four remaining squares to each of the corners, insetting each following the instructions in step 3 on page 40 as for the *Pots of Lilies Cushion*. Press toward I.

16 To make the borders, match the center point of the inner border to the center point of the middle border. Stitch in one direction.

17 Add the outer border to the middle border. Stitch in the opposite direction to stop the strip from curving. Press all seams toward the middle border.

18 To attach the borders, find the center of each side of the tablecloth and match it to the center of one long edge of each border. Pin and baste.

19 Stitch in place, easing the patchwork to the border.

20 To miter the corners follow the instructions on page 137 of the Techniques and Templates chapter.

21 For the backing, stitch a 9in/22.9cm width to each side of the full width piece.

22 Make up the quilt sandwich. *(see page 138 of the Techniques and Templates chapter)*

23 Hand quilt in-the-ditch along the piecing lines but not the main diagonals. *(see page 138 of the Techniques and Templates chapter)* Quilt around the contours of the appliqué perse shapes.

24 Trim the backing and batting level with the edges of the quilt front.

25 Prepare the binding and bind the tablecloth following the instructions on pages 137 and 138 of the Techniques and Templates chapter.

Right: *Detail of tablecloth showing one complete triangular section (left-hand side) and two half sections (top and bottom).*

Pots of Lilies Cushion

Finished size 20 x 13in/
50.8 x 33cm

MATERIALS

- Large flower print for the borders and cushion back ~ ⅔yd/60cm
- Berry print for the lilies ~ ⅛yd/10cm
- Small floral print ~ 12in/30cm
- White cotton for the lilies ~ ⅛yd/10cm
- Yellow cotton ~ 12in/30cm
- Blue cotton ~ 8in/20cm
- No 4 pre-shrunk piping cord ~ 2yd 7in/2m
- White zipper ~ 12in/30cm
- Cushion pad ~ 20 x 13in/ 51 x 33cm

CUTTING

1   From the large flower print cut two strips 2¾ x 21in/7 x 53.3cm (F) and two strips 2¾ x 14in/7 x 35.6cm (G) for the borders. Cut two pieces 11½ x 14in/29.2 x 35.6cm for the cushion back, matching the pattern.

2   From the berry print, for the lilies, cut six diamonds using template A.

3   From the small floral print, for the block surrounding the lily, cut six squares each 2⅞ x 2⅞in/7.3 x 7.3cm. Cut each in half across the diagonal to yield twelve triangles (H). Cut two strips 1½ x 4½in/3.8 x 11.4cm (I) for above the outer lily blocks, and two strips 2 x 4½in/5 x 11.4cm (J) for below the outer lily blocks. Cut one piece 3 x 4½in/7.6 x 11.4cm (K) for below the central lily block.

4   From the same, cut four sashing strips 1½ x 7in/3.8 x 17.8cm (L). For between the flower pots cut two shapes using template B. Cut one shape using template C and one shape using template C reversed.

5   From white, cut three squares each 2 x 2in/5 x 5cm. Cut each across the diagonal to yield six triangles (M) for the lily block. Cut three squares each 1⅝ x 1⅝in/2.9 x 2.9cm (N) for the top of the lily.

6   From yellow, cut six diamonds using template A for the lily petals. Cut three flower pots using template

B. To cover the piping cord, cut sufficient strips on the 45° bias to make up a length 1½ x 70in/3.8 x 177.8cm.

7   From blue, cut three triangles using template D for the base of the flowers. For the stems, cut three strips on the 45° bias 1 x 6in/2.5 x 15.2cm. Cut six leaves using template E, adding ⅛in/3mm all around for turnings.

SEWING

1   For each lily block arrange two yellow diamonds, two berry print diamonds, one blue triangle, two white triangles and one white square into a representational block.

Below: *Plan showing the components of the lily block. Right and left side flowers are identical with heads facing opposite directions.*

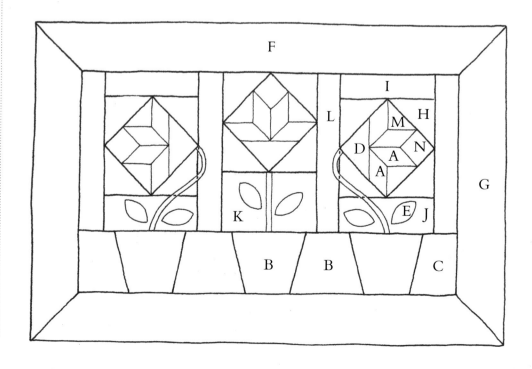

2 For the left-hand side of the lily, stitch together the yellow diamond and the berry diamond without stitching into the seam allowances.

3 Add the white triangle by pinning and stitching between the seams on one edge only. Remove the pins, re-align the fabric and stitch between the seam allowances on the second side.

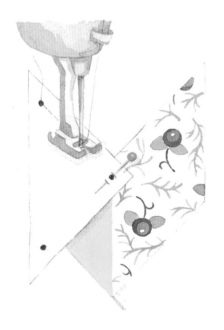

4 Make the right-hand side of the lily reversing the colors of the diamonds.

5 Stitch the two units together. Add the white square to the top and the blue triangle across the bottom.

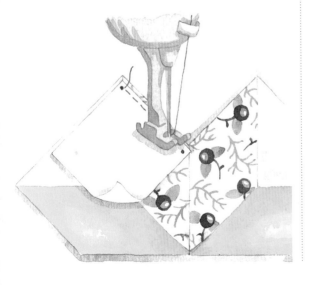

6 Stitch a floral triangle to each side of the lily block. Press the seams toward the outer triangles.

7 Stitch together the flowerpot strip as shown in the illustration below.

8 Following the instructions on page 36, stitch a straight stem to K below the central lily. Trim the ends. Stitch the stem block to the central lily.

9 Stitch the floral strips I and J above and below the outer lilies. Press the seams toward these strips. Add the sashing strips (L) to each side of these two blocks. Press the seams toward the sashing.

10 Baste the curved stems to the block. Stitch on the stems over the basting line, tucking the ends into the spaces left in the seams. Close the seams. Stitch together the three lily blocks into one panel.

11 Stitch the flowerpot strip to the lily blocks ensuring that the center of each flowerpot aligns with the center of the lily panel. Press the seam toward the flowerpots.

12 To attach the borders, find the center of one long edge of each strip and mark with a pin. On each 21in/53.3cm strip measure and mark with a pin 8in/20.3cm from each side of the center.

13 On each 14in/35.6cm strip measure and mark with a pin 4½in/11.4cm from each side of the center.

14 Find the center of each side, top and bottom of the lily panel and align each with the pins on a corresponding border strip. Pin and stitch each border in position leaving the ends overlapping.

15 Miter the corners following the instructions on page 137.

16 Appliqué the leaves following the instructions on page 134.

17 The zip is inserted vertically in the center of the back of the cushion. Follow the instructions on page 136 to insert the zip.

18 For the piping, join together sufficient 1½in/3.8cm strips to make a continuous bias length of 70in/177.8cm. *(see page 137 for Continuous Binding)* Insert the piping cord into the bias strip following the instructions on page 138.

19 To attach the piping and to make up the cushion follow the instructions on pages 138 and 136.

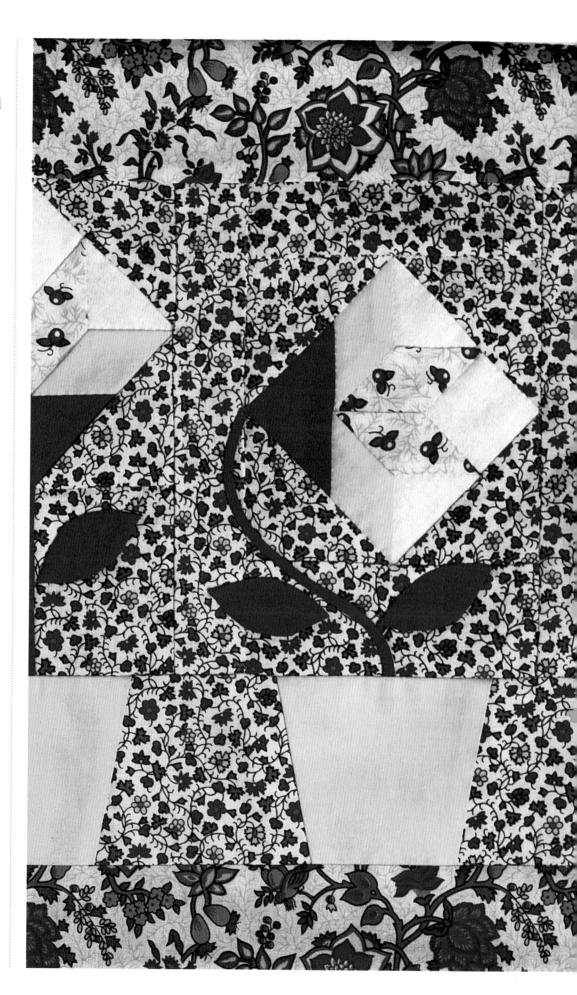

Tree of Life Panel Cushion

Finished size 18¾ x 18¾in/ 47.6 x 47.6cm

MATERIALS

- Tree of Life panel (ensuring that the panel is in the center of the length) ~ 25in/64cm
- Yellow cotton ~ 16in/40cm x 48in/122cm wide
- Yellow zipper ~ 12in/30cm
- Medium-weight iron-on interfacing ~ ¼yd/25cm
- White tissue paper

CUTTING

1 On white tissue paper draw a square 20¼ x 20¼in/51.4 x 51.4cm for the cushion front. Draw a second square inside the first, 17¼in/43.8cm, leaving a 1½in/3.8cm border all around. The second line is the foldline. Draw a third square inside the second, 15¼in/ 38.7cm leaving a 1in/2.5cm border all around. This smallest square is the stitching line.

2 Cushion back—draw a square 23¼ x 23¼in/59.1 x 59.1cm. Draw a second square 18¾in/47.6cm (the foldline) inside the first leaving a

2¼in/5.7cm border all around. Inside the second square draw a third square 15¼in/38.7cm representing the stitching line, leaving a 1¾in/4.5cm border all around.

3 Between the foldline and the outside line on the front, mark the center side points. Across each corner draw a diagonal foldline. Draw a second line parallel to the first ½in/1.3cm toward the outer edge.

4 Spread out the cushion panel on a flat surface. Center the paper design on top and pin in position. Baste along the stitching line and foldline through the tissue paper and the fabric. Mark the diagonals at the corners and the center side points. Cut out the square

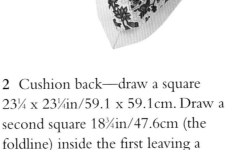

23¼in/59.1cm
18¾in/47.6cm
15¼in/38.7cm

CUSHION BACK

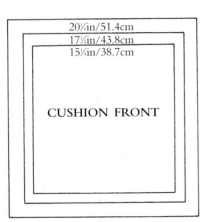

20¼in/51.4cm
17¼in/43.8cm
15¼in/38.7cm

CUSHION FRONT

and cut off the corners on the outer diagonal lines through all layers. Tear away the tissue paper leaving the basting stitches in place.

5 From the yellow, for the cushion back cut two pieces 23¼ x 12⅝in/ 59.1 x 32.1cm.

6 From the interfacing, for the cushion front, cut four strips 20 x 1½in/50.8 x 3.8cm. Cut four strips 23 x 2¼in/58.4 x 5.7cm for the cushion back.

SEWING

1 Insert the zipper in the center cushion back following the instructions on page 136. Repeat step 3 Cutting to prepare the back.

2 Pin the interfacing strips fusible side down around the edges of the wrong side of the front and back so that raw edges align. Trim the diagonal corners. Fuse the interfacing to the fabric, removing the pins as you come to them.

3 On both the front and the back, fold in the diagonal corners to the wrong side and press. Baste.

4 Turn the sides in on the foldlines. Press carefully.

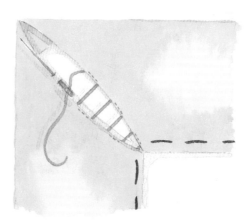

5 Ladder stitch the miters together at each corner.

6 Place the cushion back right side down on a clean flat surface. On top center the cushion front right side up.

7 From the right side of the cushion front, baste the front and back together just above and below the stitching line. Remove the original basting stitches that marked the stitching line. Sew on the stitching line, then remove all basting.

Right: Detail of red colorway of the Tree of Life panel.

Bolster Cushion

*Finished size 18 x 6 x 6in/
45.7 x 15.2 x 15.2cm*

• *Although relatively simple in
appearance, the central design requires
insetting skills and is not
recommended for an absolute beginner.*

MATERIALS

*All plain colors are based
on a fabric width of 45in/115cm*

- Blue cotton ~ 12in/30cm
- Small floral print ~ ⅛yd/10cm
- Large flower print ~ 16in/40cm
- Berry fabric ~ ⅛yd/10cm
- Floral border print ~
  24in/60cm
- Yellow cotton ~ 12in/30cm
- No 4 piping cord ~ 1⅔yd/1.5m
- Zipper ~ 12in/30cm
- Bolster cushion ~ 18in/46cm
- Two purchased tassels

CUTTING

1 From blue for the lattice design, cut
14 strips using template B, and seven
strips using template D.

2 From the small floral print, cut four
squares using template A.

3 From the large flower print cut
four squares using template A. Cut
two strips 4 x 25in/10.2 x 63.5cm for
the cushion ends.

4 From the berry print, using
template C, cut 14 triangles.

5 From the floral border print, for
the cushion, cut two strips each
20 x 7¼in/50.8 x 18.4cm.

6 From yellow, to frame the inset
patchwork, cut two strips each
20 x 1¼in/50.8 x 3.1cm. To cover the
piping cord, cut sufficient strips
1½in/3.8cm wide on the 45° bias,
joining as necessary to make up a
length 60in/152.4cm.

SEWING

• Use a ¼in/6mm seam throughout.

1 Arrange each of the fabric shapes
cut using templates A–D on a flat
surface or pinboard. *(see fig 4)*

2 Stitch the short blue strips to each
side of six squares.

3 The squares which will be pieced
to each end have one strip stitched to
one side only. Press the seams toward
the strips.

4 Stitch the berry triangles to one
short blue strip at the top of each
square. *(see fig 1)* Sew from the right-
hand side to the center mark only.

5 The gap in the line of stitching will
allow the triangle to be stitched over
the left-hand adjoining blue strip.

6 Sew a long blue strip to the right-
hand side of the square and triangle,
stitching from top to base. *(see fig 2)*

end of the triangle in the first unit away from the stitching. Stitch the loose end over the top of the adjoining long blue strip *(see fig 3)*. Repeat, alternating the large and small floral units stitching from base triangle to top to keep the patchwork straight.

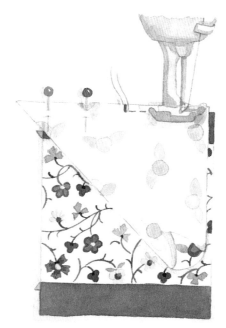

fig 1

7 Stitch a second triangle across the base. Then repeat to make eight similar units.

fig 3

9 Stitch on the end units.

10 To square-up the ends, on the wrong side of the fabric, at the intersection of the end squares, rule a line crossing the points of the two triangles and the blue strips.

11 Draw a second line parallel to the first across the outer square 1in/2.5cm away from the first line *(see fig 4)*.

12 Cut the fabric across this line.

13 Stitch the 20in/50.8cm yellow strips to each side of the lattice.

fig 2

8 Align a second unit with the left-hand side of the first. Stagger each unit so that the top of each right-hand blue strip aligns with the top horizontal blue strip. Keep the loose

fig 4

Above: View of the central lattice design.

14 Add the floral border print lengths to each side of the yellow. Trim all the ends level.

15 With right sides together, fold the patchwork in half so that the floral border print is at each end and the seams of the yellow strips and patchwork align.

16 Stitch down 3in/7.6cm at each end allowing a 1in/2.5cm seam. Leave sufficient space to insert the zip.

17 Insert the zip following the instructions on page 136 of the Techniques and Templates chapter.

18 Make sufficient continuous bias to cover the piping cord. Attach the piping to both ends of the tube following the instructions on pages 137 and 138.

19 To make the cushion ends, stitch together the short ends of the large flower print using a ½in/1.3cm seam.

20 Mark with pins the half-way and quarter points on one raw edge. Sew a long running stitch up to the marked quarter point, ⅜in/9mm from the raw edge. With a new thread sew a second row of stitches ⅛in/3mm below the first, back to the starting point.

21 Repeat on the three remaining quarters. At the opposite raw edge repeat, stitching half way around the tube, then back again, and again ⅛in/3mm underneath.

22 To attach the ends to the cushion tube, mark the quarter points of the ends of the tube, so that the seams will match those of the ends.

23 Slide the cushion ends over the tube so that right sides are together and the running stitches are toward the ends of the cushion. Match the quarter points and pin the two together.

24 Gather up the running stitches in each quarter to fit the tube, and baste the two together between the lines of running stitches and up to the piping.

25 Sew through all the layers with a piping or zipper foot.

26 Open the zip, turn the cushion to the wrong side. Pull up the gathering threads as tightly as possible in the center.

27 Secure the threads and stitch the gathers to hold. Turn right side out.

28 Stitch on a tassel in the center of the gathers.

29 Insert the cushion pad to finish.

Right: *Detail of the floral border print used for the Bolster Cushion.*

Country Basket Liner

Finished size 15½ x 12½in x 4in/
40 x 32 x 10cm

MATERIALS

- **Pelmet Vilene ~ 40in/1m of 10in/25cm width**
- **Berry fabric ~ 1⅓yd/1.2m**
- **Floral border print ~ 20in/50cm**
- **50gm/2oz batting ~ 16in/40cm square**
- **Woven wicker basket with a handle ~ 15½ x 12½ x 4in deep/40 x 32 x 10cm deep**
- **Polyester sewing thread, yellow coton à broder, embroidery floss, tapestry needle**

CUTTING

1 From Vilene, for backing the sides of the basket, cut two pieces, 15½ x 3½in/39.4 x 8.9cm, and two pieces 12½ x 3½in/31.8 x 8.9cm. Check the pieces fit comfortably inside the length and width of the basket without buckling. Trim as necessary.

2 From the berry fabric, for the basket sides cut two lengths 11in/28cm across the width of the fabric. Crosscut to yield two lengths 23½in/59.7cm, and two lengths 18½in/47cm. For backing the base, cut one piece 13½ x 16½in/34.3 x 41.9cm. Cut one piece 4 x 6in/10.2 x 15.2cm for the center panel of the basket base, and two pieces 2½ x 24in/6.4 x 61cm for the bows. Cut

and join sufficient bias strips 1¾in/4.5cm wide to make up a length 60in/152.4cm.

3 From the floral border print, cut two lengths 17½ x 5¾in/44.5 x 14.6cm and two lengths 14½ x 5¾in/36.8 x 14.6cm to surround the center panel in the base.

SEWING

- ½in/1.3cm seam allowances have been used throughout.

Basket bottom

1 To make the basket bottom, on the wrong side of the 4 x 6in/10.2 x 15.2cm berry rectangle, find and mark the centers on all four sides. With a pencil mark the ½in/1.3cm seam allowance all around.

2 On each 14½in/36.8cm floral border length, find and mark the center of one long side and the point 1½in/3.8cm to each side of the center mark.

3 On each 17½in/44.5cm length, find and mark the center point, then 2½in/6.4cm to each side of the center mark.

4 Align the center mark of each 14½in/36.8cm length with the center point of one short side of the berry rectangle. Align the

1½in/3.8cm markers with the corners on the ½in/1.3cm seam allowance.

5 With right sides together, stitch the two together between the marker pins along the 3in/7.6cm length.

6 Align the center marker and each 2½in/6.4cm marker on the 17½in/44.5cm lengths with the two remaining sides of the berry rectangle. *(see fig 1 below)*

7 Pin and stitch in position keeping the free ends of the shorter lengths away from the stitching.

8 Miter the corners following the instructions on page 137. Press.

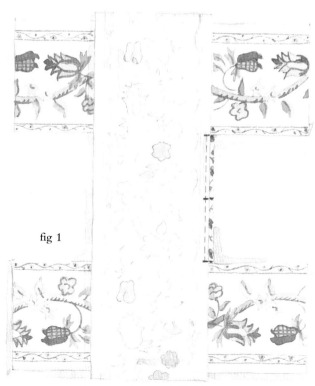

fig 1

9 Place the berry backing right side down on a clean, flat surface. Center the batting on top, then the patchwork panel right side up.

10 Pin and baste from the center outward. Quilt in-the-ditch along the seam lines.

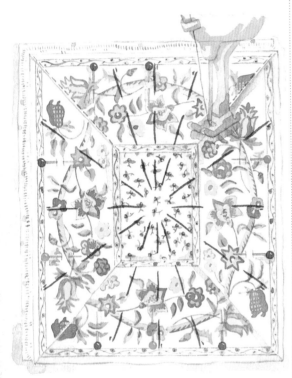

Basket sides

1 Stitch together the four berry print lengths along the 11in/27.9cm sides, alternating the 23½in/59.7cm and the 18½in/47cm lengths.

2 Fold and stitch together the two remaining 11in/27.9cm raw edges.

3 Fold the band in half wrong sides together. Sew a row of gathering stitches ½in/1.3cm below the folded edge, working from seam line to seam line through both layers of fabric. Stitch a second line below the first.

4 Sew two rows of gathering stitches ⅛in/3mm apart through one layer of

fabric at a time, 1in/2.5cm from the raw edges of both sides of the band.

5 Place the lengths of Vilene inside the four sides of the band and pin each end ¼in/6mm in from the seam.

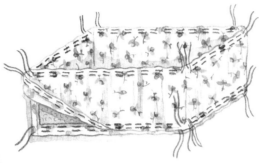

6 Gather up the stitches nearest the folded edge in each quarter of the band. These gathering stitches sit on top of the Vilene. Repeat at the other end of the band.

7 Stab stitch through the four vertical seams on the inside of the band to hold the shape, but do not sew through the Vilene.

8 Fit the side panel to the bottom, with the seams on the outside.

9 Match seam lines of the sides to the diagonal seam lines of the quilted base, rounding off the corners.

10 Stitch the sides to the base, between the rows of gathering stitches.

11 To cover the raw edges, fold the bias strip in half lengthways, wrong sides together.

12 Align the raw edges of the bias strip with the trimmed edge of the base. Stitch in place with a ¼in/6mm seam. Fold the bias tape over the

stitching line and slipstitch the folded edge in position.

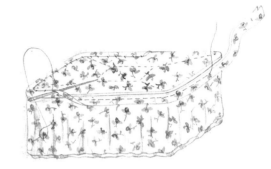

Making the bows

1 With right sides together fold each 24in/60.9cm strip in half lengthways.

2 Stitch down the length leaving a 2in/5cm opening in the center. Rotate the seam to the center of the tube and press the seam open.

3 Trim the corners diagonally. Stitch the short ends closed. Turn strips right side out through the 2in/5cm opening and ease out the corners. Slipstitch the opening shut.

4 Find the center of the strip and stitch it to the outside of the lining, inside the basket handles. Tie bows around each handle.

5 To decorate the gathered stitches at the top of the basket, loosely whip the two rows of gathered stitches with yellow embroidery floss. *(see Stitch Glossary on page 139)*

● *The instructions for the Country Basket Liner can be adapted to fit any square or rectangular basket. If you choose to use the same floral border stripe for the basket bottom, adapt the length of each measurement, keeping the width the same. Amend the dimensions of the berry rectangle. The measurements for the height and length of your basket should correspond with your new set of measurements.*

Roman Blind

Finished size 36 wide x 54in long/
91.4 x 137.2cm

MATERIALS

*Adapt the measurements to suit
your own requirements.*

- **Roman blind kit to include rings, rods, Stick & Sew strip, cords, cleat, batten, eyelets and assembly instructions**
- **Floral stripe border print ~ 20in/50cm**
- **Blue ~ 1⅔yd/1.5m**
- **Berry fabric ~ 1⅔yd/1.5m**
- **Large flower print ~ 1⅔yd/1.5m**
- **White lining fabric ~ 79in/2m**
- **Medium-weight iron-on interfacing ~ ¼yd/25cm**

CUTTING

1 From the floral stripe border print, for the decoration at the bottom of the blind, cut one shape using template A.

2 From blue, using template B, cut one shape across the width of the fabric. Cut the same from interfacing but without seam allowances. Fuse the two together following the manufacturer's instructions. For each side of the blind, on the straight grain, cut two lengths 3 x 49in/7.6 x 124.5cm. Cut one strip 2¾ x 36in/7 x 91.4cm for the rod pocket at the bottom of the blind.

3 From the berry fabric, cut one piece 30 x 49in/76.2 x 124.5cm on the straight grain.

4 From the large flower print, for the borders, on the straight grain, cut two lengths 3 x 49in/7.6 x 124.5cm.

5 From white, for the lining, cut one piece 36 x 55in/91.4 x 139.7cm. For four pockets to hide the rods, cut four strips 3½ x 36¾in/8.9 x 93.3cm.

SEWING

- Use ½in/1.3cm seam allowances throughout.

1 To make the decoration at the bottom of the blind, clip the concave edge of the blue template B almost to the stitching line. Pin shapes A and B together, matching centers and dots. Stitch together and press the seam toward the blue.

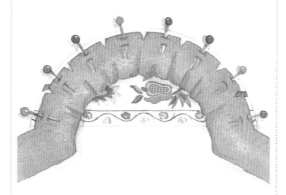

2 To make the right-hand border of the blind, place the 3in/7.6cm wide blue length on top of the shorter large flower print, aligning raw edges at the top short end. Pin, then stitch from top to bottom so that the blue is on the outside. Reverse the fabrics for the left-hand border. Press the seams open. Stitch the borders to each side of the berry fabric, ensuring that the colors run in the correct sequence and the stitching runs from top to bottom. Press the seams open.

3 Find the center of the bottom of the blind and match it to the center of the curved blind decoration. Place right sides together. Pin, stitch and press the seam toward the decoration. Miter the corners following the instructions on page 137.

4 Find and mark with pins the top and bottom centers of the blind and the lining. On a clean, flat surface spread out the blind right side up. On top, place the curtain lining right side down. Align raw edges at the right-hand side. Pin, then stitch from top to bottom. *(see fig 1 on next page)*

5 Repeat, aligning the left-hand raw edges. Notice that the lining is 1in/2.5cm narrower. Turn the tube right side out and match the center marking pins.

6 Iron from the center outward: ½in/1.3cm of the blue border will wrap around to the back of the blind on each side. Baste ½in/1.3cm in from the seam lines on both sides, down the center and across the top of the blind. Baste along the bottom edge

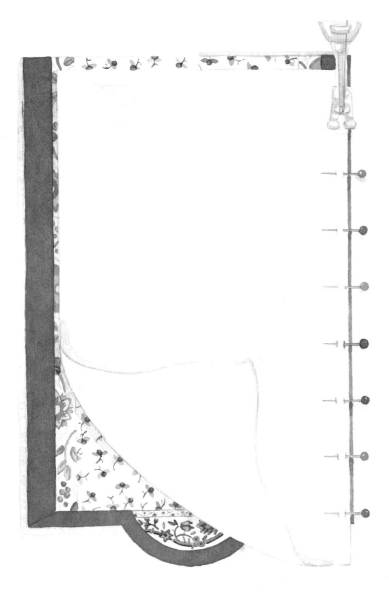

fig 1

12 Trim the lining at the bottom of the blind to the shape of the curved decoration. Remove the basting stitches. Turn in ½in/1.3cm of blue fabric to the wrong side, clipping where necessary. Stitch in position to the interfacing only, so that the stitching does not show on the right side of the blind. Turn in ¼in/6mm of lining, clipping as necessary. Baste, then slipstitch in place to the blue seam allowance only. Press.

13 Make the blue pocket for the bottom of the blind. Turn in ½in/1.3cm on each raw edge and press. Slipstitch the bottom of the strip to the wrong side of the blind ¼in/6mm up from the straight edges and across the top of the curved decoration. Insert the rod, then pin the top of the strip in position. Carefully remove the rod, then baste and stitch in position through the lining only. Replace the rod and stitch down the short ends.

following the curved line. Do not cut away the excess lining.

7 To mark the position of the rods, spread out the blind on a flat surface. On the lining, draw a horizontal line ½in/1.3cm from the top of the blind, then 12½in/31.8cm, then at 10in/25.4cm intervals.

8 For the pockets to hide the rods, turn in ⅜in/1cm on each 3½in/8.9cm end of the white strips only. Press. Fold the strips in half lengthways and press. Open out the center fold, then turn in the raw edges to the center line and press. Fold in half again on the foldline, press.

9 Attach the pockets, to the wrong side of the blind. Pin the open edges of the pockets to the marked horizontal lines. Ignore the ½in/1.3cm line at the top.

10 Stitch each in position through all the layers using matching thread and changing the bobbin thread where necessary. (see fig 2)

11 Trim the rods ⅜in/1cm shorter than the pocket width. Insert the rods in the pockets then stitch down the ends enclosing the rods.

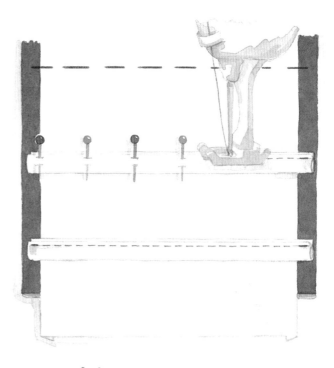

fig 2

14 To stitch on the rings, on each pocket measure and mark a point 2¾in/7cm from each side of the blind. Mark the center of each pocket. Stitch three rings to the bottom edges of the pockets.

15 At the top of the blind, turn the raw edges in using a ½in/1.3cm seam. Align the "sew" side of the Stick & Sew strip with the top of the wrong side of the blind. Pin and stitch in position along each edge.

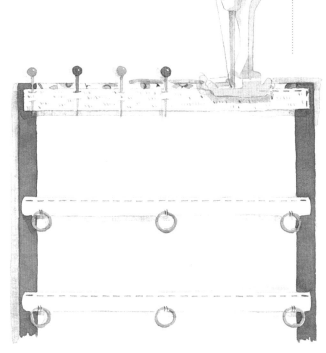

16 Refer to the manufacturer's instructions to insert the cords in the blind and to attach the batten and eyelets.

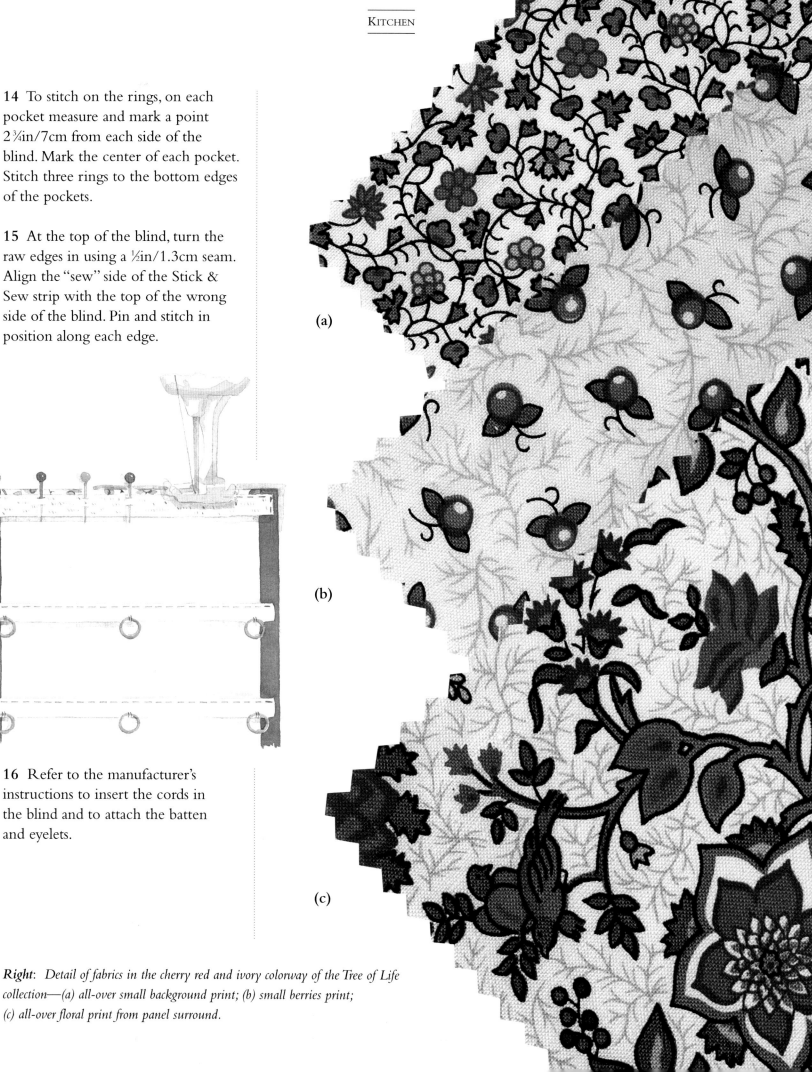

(a)

(b)

(c)

Right: Detail of fabrics in the cherry red and ivory colorway of the Tree of Life collection—(a) all-over small background print; (b) small berries print; (c) all-over floral print from panel surround.

Dining Room

"The Dining Room as we know it is an innovation in house planning. In the early Middle Ages the noble and his retainers took meals together in the Hall; subsequently the 'grande salle,' built for ceremonial uses, began to be used as a banqueting room, while the private repasts were served in the lord's chamber. In many old English house plans we find rooms designated as 'dining parlours,' though these can hardly be said to represent our modern dining-room, since they were not planned in connection with the Kitchen and offices; still, it is from the Elizabethan dining parlour that the modern dining room has developed."

From The Liberty Handbook of Sketches—A catalog of interior designs & furnishing.

~Pinboard for the Dining Room Chairs and Drape ~

The pinboard displays three different loose cover designs for dining room chairs with my fabric choices.

I wanted the dining room to reflect some of the views held by many distinguished late-Victorian artists, architects and dilettantes. To this end I have incorporated in the projects their passion for the Neo-gothic style as exemplified by Pugin and the heraldic vision of chivalry and baronial castles as championed by novelist and antiquarian Sir Walter Scott. Scott's great achievement was his home Abbotsford in Scotland. At great expense he transformed a modest Scottish farmhouse into a most remarkable and influential baronial hall and filled it with ancient curiosities and armor.

I also kept in mind Robert Kerr's words from his 1864 publication of *The Gentleman's House*, in which he recommends that dining room furnishings be "somewhat massive and simple" and "that the whole appearance of the room ought to be that of masculine importance."

1 Lozenge print from the *Napier* collection in various colorways

2 Stripe in various colorways from the *Napier* collection

3 Textured stripe

4 Tana lawn, small all-over floral print *(Capel)* in red and blue colorways

5 Acanthus leaf design in green colorway from the *Vittoria* collection

6 Neo-gothic Puginesque architecture

7 Fleur-de-lis motifs for stencil work, wallpaper

8 Heraldic motifs

9 Appliqué work

10 Decorative tassels and fringing

Fleur-de-lis Chair Cover

MATERIALS

*Read the Measuring and Cutting
section to estimate your material
requirements.*

- Green stripe for the chair seat
- Heavy-weight muslin for both
  sides of the chair back
- Blue and red stripe for the skirt
  and piping
- Lining for the skirt
- Batting for the chair back
- Fabric scraps for the appliqué
  motifs
- Red, and blue six-stranded
  embroidery floss
- Scraps of fusible webbing
- Piping cord

MEASURING AND CUTTING

1 Make a paper template of the chair
back. Check the thickness of the
chair, measuring the widest part. Add
seams. Cut one on the straight grain.

2 For the decorative front, make a
second template adding double this
measurement at both sides. Add
½in/1.3cm on all four sides for seams.
Cut one on the straight grain.

3 For the batting, the length is the
height of the chair back from the seat
to the top + the thickness + 6in/
15.2cm to wrap over the top of the
chair. The width is the maximum
width of the chair.

4 Make a paper template of the chair
seat. Add ½in/1.3cm seams on all
sides. Cut one from fabric on the
straight grain.

5 Length of the skirt and lining—
Measure the circumference of the
frame at seat level. Add to your
measurement 14in/35.6cm for each
corner for the pleats. For the width,
measure the drop from the seat to the
floor. Add 1in/2.5cm for seams. Cut
one from lining and one from blue
and red stripe.

6 Piping—Measure the front and
sides of the seat. Measure the sides
and top of the chair back. Make
1½in/3.8cm wide continuous
binding, 6in/15.2cm longer than each
measurement. *(see page 137)*

7 Using the template on page 142,
bond and cut one fleur-de-lis motif
from fabric scraps and put aside.
Follow the instructions on page 134
of Techniques and Templates.

SEWING

- ½in/1.3cm seams have been used
  throughout.

Skirt

1 With right sides together, stitch the
two short ends together to make a
tube. Repeat with the lining. Press.

2 With right sides together fit the
lining inside the skirt, aligning raw
edges and seams. Pin, then stitch
along one long edge only. Turn right
side out.

3 Ease 1in/2.5cm of blue and red
stripe onto the lining side to form a
hem and press with a damp cloth.
Trim the excess lining at the other

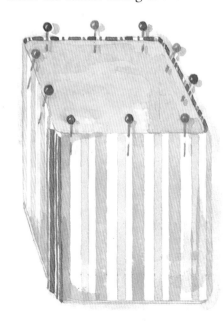

raw edge level with the blue and red stripe. With pins, divide the skirt in half, then in four, then in eight. Put to one side.

Chair back

1   Center the fleur-de-lis motif on the right side of one piece of cream fabric and fuse in place. Machine satin stitch around the outline.

2   Add the scroll in running stitch using six strands of blue embroidery floss. Add French knots using six strands of red embroidery floss. *(see page 68)*

3   Make up the piping following the instructions on page 138 of the Techniques and Templates chapter.

4   Pin the piping around the sides and top only of the chair back, aligning all raw edges. Baste and stitch in place, using a zipper foot, close to the cord.

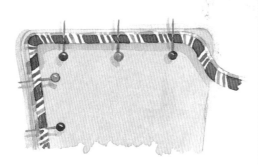

5   With right sides together, align raw edges. At the top, find the center of the back and front, match points and pin together. Pin the top outward from the center, pushing the excess up to the seam allowance.

6   Pinch the excess into a dart and hand stitch, then fold in and pin the dart to the top seam. Baste. Try the chair back on the chair. Adjust seams

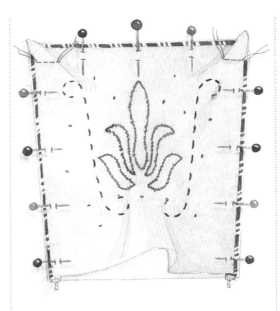

to fit. Pin and stitch the back and front together close to the piping using a zipper foot.

7   Starting at the bottom, fit the batting to the chair front and over the seam at the top to the chair back. Taper to fit. Hold in place with a few stitches in the seam at each side. Turn right side out. Put to one side.

Chair seat

1   Baste the piping to the right side of the chair seat, around both sides and the front only. Stitch in place close to the piping.

2   To fit the chair seat to the chair back, place right sides together. Align the raw edges of the center of the back of the seat with the center of the base of the front. Pin and stitch. Some of the front may project beyond the seat fabric on both sides.

Fitting the skirt to the chair seat

1   To fit the skirt to the chair seat and chair back, turn the skirt lining side out. Align the raw edge of the skirt with the raw edge of the chair back and seat. The skirt will go around the outside of the chair back.

2   Align each of the quarter marker pins on the skirt with a corner of the chair seat. Find the middle of the sides of the seat and align with the remaining pins.

3   Pleat the excess fabric into the corners. Baste securely. Turn right side out and check the fit.

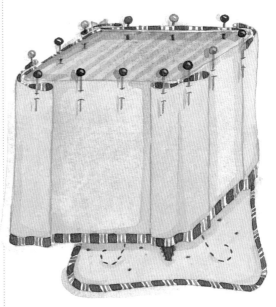

4   Stitch the skirt in place using the zipper foot on the sewing machine.

Fleur-de-lis Drape

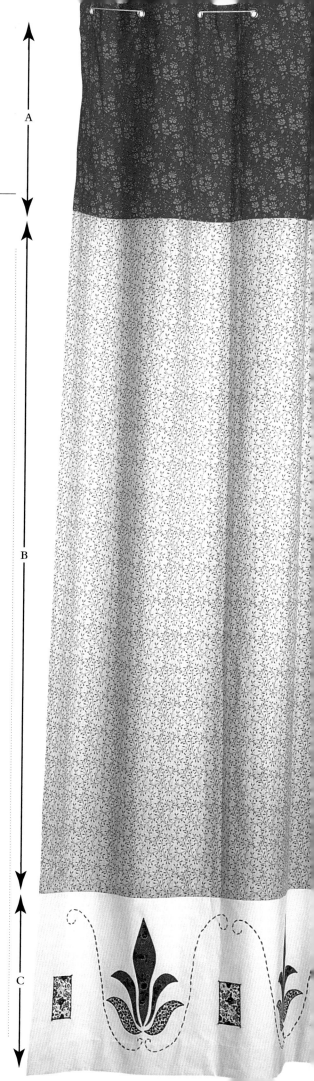

Finished size 78 x 48½in/ 198.1 x 123.2cm

MATERIALS

- Red floral print for the top of the drape (A) ~ 1⅛yd/1m
- Tan leaf print for the drape (B) ~ 3yd/2.6m
- Cream for the bottom of the drape (C) ~ ¾yd/60cm of 60in/152cm wide muslin or cotton
- Lining 2¼yd/2.1m of 60in/152cm wide fabric
- Fabric scraps for the appliqué motifs
- Medium-weight Vilene for the drape top to punch the eyelets into
- Nine metal eyelets ~ ¾in/2cm diameter
- Scraps of fusible web
- Two round weights for the bottom of the drape
- Blue six-stranded embroidery floss

CUTTING

- ½in/1.3cm seams have been used throughout.

1 For A, cut the length in half to yield two pieces 20in/50.8cm long. Remove the selvages. With right sides together, sew along one 20in/50.8cm edge. Press the seam open. Cut to make one piece 20 x 52½in/50.8 x 133.4cm.

2 For B, from tan leaf print, cut the piece in half to yield two pieces 1½yd/1.3m long. Remove the selvages. With right sides together, sew along one selvage edge. Press the seam open and cut to make one piece 50½ x 52½in/128.3 x 133.4cm.

3 For C, cut one piece 18¼ x 52½in/ 45.7 x 133.4cm.

4 From lining cut one piece 48½ x 80½in/123.2 x 204.5cm.

5 Read the Techniques and Templates chapter for instructions on making templates and using fusible web and appliqué. Bond and cut three fleur-de-lis motifs from fabric scraps for the bottom of the drape.

6 Bond and cut four rectangles 2¼ x 3¼in/5.7 x 8.3cm.

SEWING

1 Mark the hemline fold 4¼in/ 10.8cm up from the lower raw edge of the cream fabric. On a flat surface on the right side of the cream fabric, position each of the appliqué motifs in the remaining area. When you are happy with the arrangement remove

Right: *Detail of Fleur-de-lis Drape indicating the main components: (A) a top band of red floral print; (B) leaf print for the body of the drape; and (C) the appliqué border hem. The drape is hung using a yacht wire threaded through the eyelets.*

the paper backing from the fusible web and bond each in place following the manufacturer's instructions.

2 Machine satin stitch around each of the motifs.

3 Using six strands of blue embroidery floss and long running stitch sew the scroll pattern around the fleur-de-lis motifs.

4 With right sides together, and raw edges aligned, pin and stitch the fleur-de-lis panel to the bottom of the tan print, ensuring that the motifs are the correct way up.

5 Press the seam toward the tan leaf print.

6 To the top of B, with right sides together, pin and stitch the red floral print. *(see top of column 2)* Press the seam toward the tan leaf print.

7 Turn in 2in/5cm at each side of the drape and press. Open out the folds.

8 Turn in 2in/5cm at the hemline of C and press. Turn in a further 2¼in/5.7cm and press.

9 Make a fabric pocket to hold the weights so that they do not discolor the fabric. Follow the instructions at step 6 Drape, of the *Patchwork Drape* on page 88.

10 Miter the two bottom corners of the drape only following the instructions for the *Patchwork Drape* on page 88.

11 Stitch the fabric pocket to the lining close to the seam allowance to hold the weights securely in place.

12 Stitch the miter enclosing the weights at each corner.

13 At the drape top, turn in 2in/5cm, press. Turn in another 2in/5cm. Press. Open out the folds.

Lining

1 Prepare the lining by turning in 1in/2.5cm at each side and press.

2 At the bottom turn in 2in/5cm, press. Turn in another 2in/5cm. Press, and stitch.

3 Open out the folds at the top only.

4 Place the strip of Vilene between the two foldlines and baste in place without knotting the thread ends.

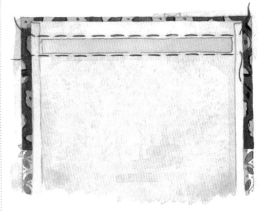

5 With right sides together and raw edges aligned, center the top of the lining along the top of the drape. Pin and stitch in place. Press.

6 Turn right side out and refold on the foldlines.

7 Baste and slipstitch the folded edge of the lining to the turned-in edge of the drape at each side only.

8 Slipstitch the folded red floral print at the top to the lining along the folded edge of red.

9 Arrange the eyelets along the top of the drape, ½in/1.3cm from the top, and equally spaced across the width of the drape.

10 Attach each following the manufacturer's instructions.

11 Remove the basting stitches.

Pinboard for the Dining ~ Room Tablecloth ~

The pinboard displays the many elements used for the tablecloth project. Several tablecoth designs are included and each incorporates part of the main fleur-de-lis motif. Each design distinguishes the two main design areas—the square flat surface of the tabletop and the border drop. Each tablecloth has a different border and binding treatment—prairie points (A), pompoms (B), silk ribbon tassels (C), and machine-embroidered lace (D). The center square should measure the size of your tabletop.

1 Dainty leaf print *(Briarwood)* in tan and ivory colorways

2 Acanthus leaf print *(Vittoria)* in blue colorway

3 Tana lawn *(Clarissanne)*

4 Stripe from the *Napier* collection

5 Paisley from the *Umritza* collection

6 Stylized paisley floral from the *Napier* collection

7 Delicate berries *(Voysey)* in green and yellow colorway

8 Trailing flower motif on a textured ground from the *Napier* collection

9 Fleur-de-lis motifs for stencil work, wallpaper

10 Appliqué work

11 Silk ribbon work

12 French knots

13 Decorative tassels and fringing

Fleur-de-lis Tablecloth

Finished size 42 x 42in/
106.7 x 106.7cm

MATERIALS

- **Fine white cotton for the tablecloth and backing ~ 2½yd/2.2m**
- **Red fabric scraps for the fleur-de-lis motifs**
- **Scraps of fusible webbing for the appliqué motifs**
- **Red, and blue six-stranded embroidery floss**
- **Green and yellow berry fabric for the tablecloth center and appliqué motifs ~ ¾yd/60cm**
- **Red floral to edge the central square ~ ⅛yd/10cm**
- **Red and blue stripe for the binding ~ ⅛yd/10cm**

CUTTING

1 For the tablecloth and backing, cut two squares 42 x 42in/106.7 x 106.7cm.

2 For the appliqué center, cut one square 19 x 19in/48.3 x 48.3cm.

3 From the red floral, cut and join straight grain strips 1in/2.5cm wide to make one continuous length of edging 80 x 1in/200 x 2.5cm.

4 Read the Techniques and Templates chapter for instructions on making templates and appliqué using fusible webbing. Bond and cut eight fleur-de-lis motifs.

5 For the binding, cut and join strips 1in/2.5cm wide to make one strip 176in/4.5m long.

SEWING

- Use a ¼in/6mm seam allowance unless otherwise stated.

1 On one piece of white fabric, find the center point, by folding the square in half in both directions.

2 Press lightly with an iron. Open out the folds.

3 Make a paper template of an 18in/45.7cm square and find the center point.

4 With the tablecloth right side up, match the center point of the paper square to the center point of the tablecloth and pin the two together.

5 With a fabric marker and ruler, lightly draw the outline of the paper square on the tablecloth, then remove

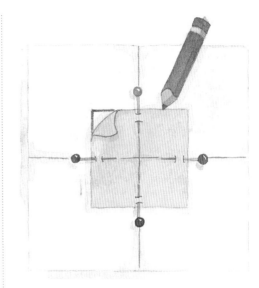

the template. The drawn line is the stitching line for the red floral edging.

6 Prepare the red floral edging by folding the strip in half lengthways, wrong sides together and press.

7 Beginning part way along one side of the drawn square on the tablecloth, place the red floral edging on the drawn line as shown below. Have the fold ⅛in/3mm outside the pencil line

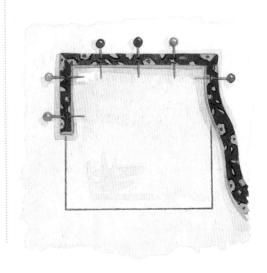

and the raw edges toward the center of the tablecloth.

8　Miter the edging at the corners. *(see page 137 for mitering corners)*

9　Trim the red floral strip 1in/2.5cm longer than required. Turn in a small seam allowance at the short raw edge. Remove the pins from the beginning of the strip and slip the short raw edge inside the turning. Pin in position. Sew the edging in place.

10　Turn in ½in/1.3cm on all sides of the center square, mitering the corners. Press carefully.

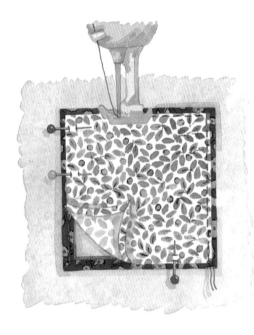

11　Fit the square into the center of the red floral edging so that the folded edge just covers the previous stitching line. Pin and stitch in place.

Adding the appliqués

1　Position each of the motifs 2½in/6.4cm from the raw edges of the tablecloth—one at each corner and one in the center of each side.

2　Lightly mark the scroll pattern with a pencil to ensure that it fits.

3　When you are happy with the arrangement, remove the paper backing and fuse in place following the manufacturer's instructions.

4　Using appropriate color thread, machine satin stitch around the raw edge of each motif.

Assembling the tablecloth

1　Place the backing right side down on a clean, flat surface. Smooth out any wrinkles.

2　On top place the tablecloth right side up. Pin the two together.

3　In the seam allowance, work a round of permanent basting.

Finishing

1　With six strands of blue embroidery floss and using running stitch, embroider the scroll pattern through both layers of the tablecloth.

2　Add random-stitched French knots around the fleur-de-lis motifs using red embroidery floss.

3　Working from the back of the tablecloth, bring the needle through both layers of fabric to the front. Wrap the thread around the needle twice. *(fig 1)* Insert the needle back at the start point. Holding the thread taut, pull the needle through the loops to the back of the work. *(fig 2)*

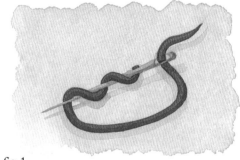

fig 1

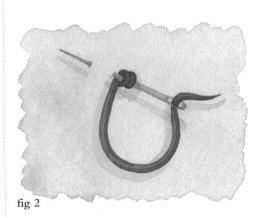

fig 2

4　Bind the tablecloth following the instructions on page 138 of the Techniques and Templates chapter, to finish ¼in/6mm wide. Miter the corners as you come to them.

Fleur-de-lis Napkin

Finished size 14¼ x 14¼in/ 36.2 x 36.2cm

MATERIALS

For one napkin you will need:
- Fine white cotton ~ 15in/40cm square
- Sheer white fabric to back the napkin ~ 15in/40cm square
- Binding ~ ⅛ yd/10cm
- Fabric scraps for the motifs
- Scraps of fusible webbing
- Red, and blue six-stranded embroidery floss
- Matching machine embroidery thread

CUTTING

1 Read the Techniques and Templates chapter for instructions on making templates and appliqué using fusible webbing. Bond and cut one fleur-de-lis motif.

2 From fine cotton for the napkin, cut one square 14¼ x 14¼in/36.8 x 36.8cm. Cut the same from the sheer white fabric for backing.

3 For binding, make up a length of continuous binding 1in/2.5cm wide x 62in/157.5cm long. *(see page 137)*

SEWING

- Use ¼in/6mm seam allowance.

1 Arrange the templates on the right side of one corner of the napkin, 1in/ 2.5cm from the raw edges. Lightly draw around the motifs with a pencil to mark the position of each.

2 Remove the backing from the motifs and fuse in position. Machine satin stitch around each shape. Press.

3 Place the cotton napkin right side down. On top place the sheer fabric. Pin together. Work a line of permanent basting around the raw edges within the ¼in/6mm seam.

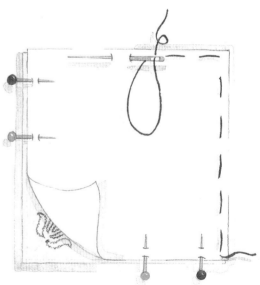

4 Embroider the scroll shape around the fleur-de-lis through both layers using running stitch. Add French knots in red embroidery floss.

5 Taking a ¼in/6mm seam, bind the napkin, mitering the corners. Follow the instructions on page 137 of Techniques and Templates.

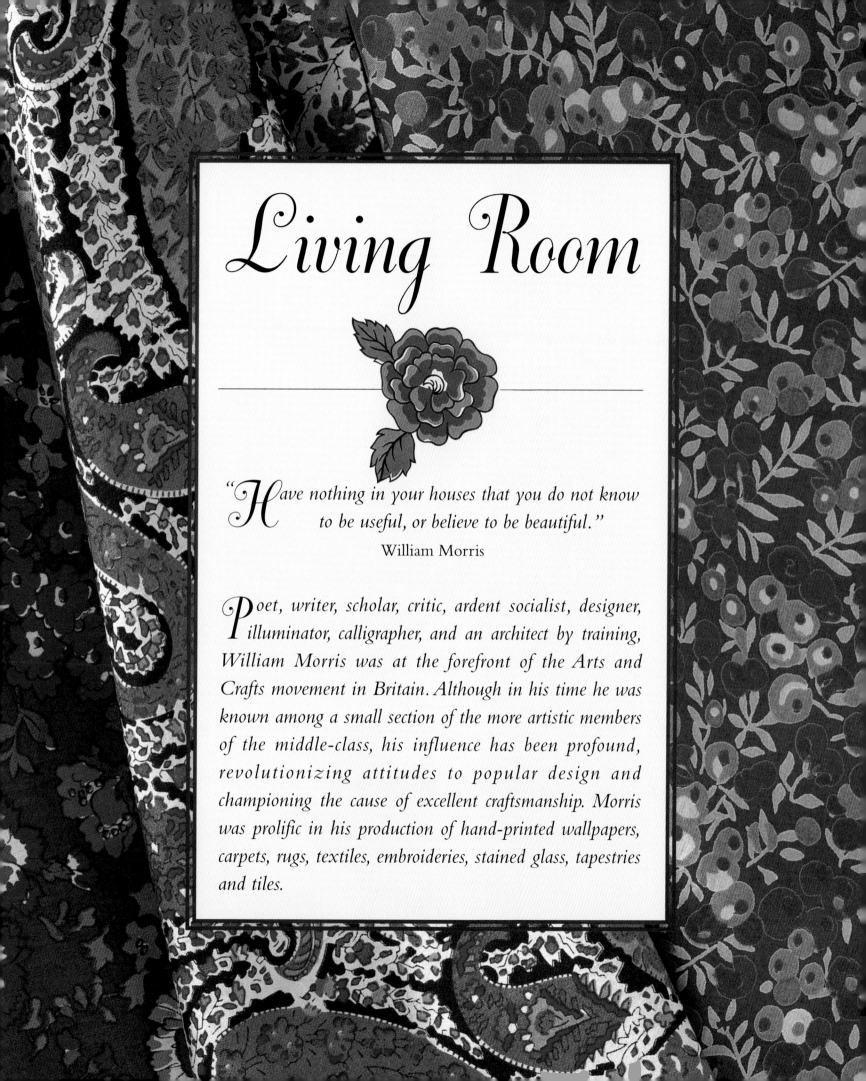

Living Room

"Have nothing in your houses that you do not know to be useful, or believe to be beautiful."

William Morris

Poet, writer, scholar, critic, ardent socialist, designer, illuminator, calligrapher, and an architect by training, William Morris was at the forefront of the Arts and Crafts movement in Britain. Although in his time he was known among a small section of the more artistic members of the middle-class, his influence has been profound, revolutionizing attitudes to popular design and championing the cause of excellent craftsmanship. Morris was prolific in his production of hand-printed wallpapers, carpets, rugs, textiles, embroideries, stained glass, tapestries and tiles.

Pinboard for the Living Room ~

The pinboard displays the many fabrics and trims that served to inspire the projects for the Living Room.

William Morris and the principles of the Arts and Crafts movement have had a considerable impact on our perception of Liberty style and as a tribute I have chosen the *Strawberry Thief* as the main motif for the Living Room. The cheeky bird, originally designed by Morris, appears in several guises on a cushion panel and as a cut-out on a lampshade.

The fabrics chosen for the projects are from the *Briarwood* collection in the rose and emerald on tea-colored ground colorway. I have combined this lovely collection with a patchwork of colorful Tana lawn florals.

1 Panel print *(Briarwood)*

2 Dainty leaf print *(Briarwood)*

3 Hedgerow motifs

4 *Vittoria* stripe/border design

5 Acanthus leaf all-over design *(Vittoria)*

6 Tana lawn *(Wiltshire)*

7 Tana lawn *(Glenjade)*

8 Tana lawn *(Camilla)*

9 Tana lawn *(Sophine)*

10 Tana lawn *(Clarissanne)*

11 Tana lawn *(Bourton)*

12 Tana lawn *(Thorpe)*

13 Tana lawn *(Strawberry Thief)*

14 Simple block patchwork

15 Sun-ray motif from the *Napier* collection

16 Decorative fringing and trims

Briarwood Panel Cushion

Finished size 20½ x 20½in/
52.1 x 52.1cm

MATERIALS

- Two cushion panels ~
  ½yd/50cm
- Leaf border print ~ 1¼yd/1.2m
- 100gm/4oz batting ~
  ¼yd/25cm
- Braid to decorate the front ~
  1½yd/1.4m
- Zipper ~ 12in/30cm
- Cushion pad ~ 16 x 16in/
  40 x 40cm

CUTTING

1 For the front, cut one panel,
centering the motif in a square 16 x
16in/40.6 x 40.6cm. For the back cut
one panel 16 x 18in/40.6 x 45.7cm
allowing extra length to insert the
zipper and provide a concealed zip.

2 From the border print, cut eight
lengths 21 x 3½in/53.4 x 8.9cm.

3 From the batting, for the borders,
cut four lengths 21 x 2½in/53.4
x 6.4cm.

SEWING

- Use ½in/1.3cm seams throughout.

1 For the cushion back, turn in
½in/1.3cm along one long edge of
each border strip and press. Open out
the fold. With right sides together, raw
edges aligned, and the pressed foldline

toward the raw edge, center one
border at the top of the panel. Pin.

2 Insert the zipper following the
instructions on page 136. Stitch the
border in place to the cushion back
only following the instructions in Step
2 of the *Vittoria Border Cushion*.

3 Miter the corners following the
instructions in Steps 3 and 4 of the
Vittoria Border Cushion.

4 For the cushion front, if the braid is
to be sewn into the seam do so at this

point. Beginning at one corner baste
the braid to the raw edge of the
center panel so that the finished edge
is toward the seam and the loose
thread ends are toward the center of
the cushion. At the corners pleat the
fabric into a mock miter. As you
return to the beginning trim the braid
slightly longer than required and
overlap the two edges. Add the
cushion borders.

5 Make up the cushion following
steps 11–16 of the *Vittoria Border
Cushion* on page 77.

Vittoria Border Cushion

Finished size 20½ x 20½in/
52.1 x 52.1cm

MATERIALS

- Leaf print for the center panel ~ ½yd/50cm
- Border print ~ ¾yd/70cm
- 4oz/100gm batting ~ ¼yd/25cm
- Braid to decorate the front ~ 1½yd/1.4m
- Zipper ~ 12in/30cm
- Cushion pad ~ 16 x 16in/ 40 x 40cm

CUTTING

1 From the leaf print, for the cushion front, cut one piece 12½ x 12½in/ 31.7 x 31.7cm.

2 For the cushion back, cut one piece 12½ x 6½in/31.7 x 16.5cm, and one piece 12½ x 7in/31.7 x 17.8cm.

3 From the border print, cut four lengths 21½ x 5½in/54.6 x 14cm.

4 From batting, for the borders, cut four lengths 21½ x 2in/54.6 x 5cm.

SEWING

- ½in/1.3cm seams have been used throughout.

1 Insert the zipper in the back center panel using ½in/1.3cm seams and following the instructions on page 136 of Techniques and Templates.

2 Turn in ½in/1.3cm along one long edge of each border strip and press. Open out the fold. With right sides together, raw edges aligned, and the pressed foldline toward the raw edge, center one border at one side of the panel. Pin. Stitch the border in place beginning ½in/1.3cm from the raw edge of the center panel, and stopping ½in/1.3cm from the end of the center panel. Press. Add a border to the opposite side. Pin and stitch the two remaining borders to the center panel in the same way.

3 Refold the ½in/1.3cm seam allowance along each border strip at the corner overlaps. At the corners, fold back the excess fabric along each border to the point where the stitching commences and lightly fingerpress. Open out the folds one at a time. *(see drawing top of column 3)*

4 Fold a diagonal at a 45° angle at each corner, radiating out from the point where the stitching commences to the raw edges. Lightly fingerpress. The excess border will align with the first fingerpressed fold. Repeat on the second border.

5 Fold the cushion back diagonally right sides together, and align the miter folds in the border. Pin and baste across the folded corner. Check that the miter is true and lies flat.

6 Machine stitch in place. Repeat at each corner.

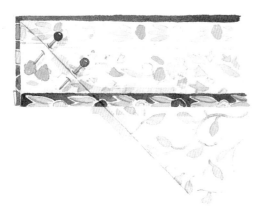

7 Add the borders to the center front panel in the same way.

8 Begin at one corner and baste the braid along the seam line of the front center panel and border.

9 At the corners pleat the fabric into a mock miter.

10 Trim the braid slightly longer than required and turn in the raw edge. Sew in place.

11 Place the cushion back and front right sides together, aligning raw edges. Undo the zipper. Stitch the two pieces together using a ½in/1.3cm seam allowance. Turn right side out and press.

12 With the cushion inside out, trim the short ends of the batting at 45° angles to match the miters at the stitching line joining the back and front of the cushion together.

13 Baste the batting to the cushion front only aligning the outer edge with the stitching line. Use large stitches and do not knot the thread end. Repeat on all four sides. Turn the cushion right side out. *(see fig 1)*

14 On the cushion front, with basting, mark out the 16in/40.6cm square in the center of the cushion. *(see fig 2)* Try the cushion pad for fit, adjusting the basting stitches as necessary.

15 On the right side of the fabric, machine stitch around the outline of basting stitches. Remove all basting.

16 Insert the cushion pad to finish.

fig 1

fig 2

Strawberry Thief Cushion

Finished size 19½ x 19½in/
49.5 x 49.5cm

MATERIALS

- *Strawberry Thief* Tana lawn for
  the appliqué panels ~ ½yd/50cm
- Blue sun-ray print ~ ¾yd/70cm
- Braid to decorate the cushion
  front 1¾yd/1.6m

- Cushion pad ~ 16 x 16in/
  40 x 40cm
- Zipper ~ 14in/35cm
- 4oz/100gm batting ~
  ¼yd/25cm
- Four self-cover buttons
- Scraps of blue fabric to cover
  the buttons

CUTTING

1 From the *Strawberry Thief* print,
cut one piece 14½ x 14½in/36.8 x
36.8cm for the cushion front. For the
cushion back, cut one piece 4¾ x
14½in/12.1 x 36.8cm, and one piece
11 x 14½in/27.9 x 36.8cm.

2 From the blue sun-ray print, for the
cushion front, cut one piece

20½ x 20½in/52.1 x 52.1cm. For the cushion back, cut one piece 7½ x 20½in/19.1 x 52.1cm, and one piece 13½ x 20½in/34.3 x 52.1cm.

3 From the batting, cut four strips 20½ x 1½in/52.1 x 3.8cm.

SEWING

● ½in/1.3cm seams have been used throughout, unless otherwise stated.

1 Turn in ¼in/6mm around the raw edges of the *Strawberry Thief* print for the cushion front only. Press.

2 For the cushion front, on the sun-ray 20½in/52.1cm square, baste 3¼in/8.3cm from each raw edge.

3 Position the center panel inside the basting lines, then machine stitch the panel in place, as close to the folded edge of the center panel as possible.

4 For the cushion back, place the two pieces, side by side, right side up on a flat surface, aligning the 14½in/ 36.8cm edges. The two aligned edges

are not turned in at this stage. On the remaining edges of each piece, turn in ¼in/6mm.

5 Baste 3¼in/8.3cm from two short edges and one long edge on each piece of the cushion back.

6 Position the smaller panel on the 7½in/19.1cm sun-ray print, so that the raw edge of the panel aligns with the raw edge of the sun-ray print.

7 Pin and stitch close to the folded edges, and within the seam allowance along the long raw edge. Repeat for the remaining piece.

8 Insert the zipper in the center back, taking ½in/1.3cm seam and following the instructions on page 136 of the Techniques and Templates chapter.

fig 1

Above: Twisting strands together.

9 Stitch the braid to the cushion front. Beginning 3in/7.6cm from the corner, baste the braid in position around the seamline of the center panel, covering the point where the two fabrics meet.

10 As you return to the beginning, trim the cord so that it is slightly longer than the start point.

11 Undo the cord and twist the strands together. *(see fig 1)*

12 Hand stitch the braid in place as invisibly as possible.

13 Make up the cushion and insert the batting following the instructions for the *Vittoria Border Cushion*.

14 Cover four self-cover buttons following the manufacturer's instructions.

15 Attach one to each corner of the *Strawberry Thief* central panel.

Lap Quilt

*Finished size 60 x 60in/
152.4 x 152.4cm*

MATERIALS

- Cream print for the background of the Tree of Life block (A) ~ 1yd/80cm
- Printed background (B) ~ ½yd/40cm
- *Briarwood* (C) ~ 12in/30cm
- Print (D) ~ ¼yd/20cm
- ¼yd/20cm each of seven mixed prints for the tree and outer border (X)
- Print (E) for the tree trunks ~ ⅛yd/10cm
- Floral border stripe for corner units and filling in triangles (F) ~ ½yd/50cm
- Orange floral print for the inner border (G) ~ ½yd/40cm
- Black leaf-on-cream background for the middle and sawtooth borders (H) ~ 1½yd/1.3m
- Backing ~ 3½yd/3.1m
- Binding ~ ¾yd/65cm
- Batting ~ 1¾yd/1.6m

CUTTING

Steps 1–6 give cutting instructions for the 13 Tree of Life blocks. As you cut each piece label it with the measurement. Divide the total number of squares equally into 13 and keep each block separate.

Right: Detail of some of the fabrics used in the Lap Quilt.

1 From the cream background A, cut 52 squares 2⅞in/7.3cm for the Tree of Life blocks. Cut 13 squares 2½in/6.4cm and 13 squares 6½in/16.5cm.

2 From B, cut 13 squares 2½in/6.4cm. Cut 39 squares 2⅞in/7.3cm.

3 From *Briarwood* C, cut 39 squares 2½in/6.4cm for the Tree of Life blocks.

4 From print D, cut 20 squares 2⅞in/7.3cm.

5 From each of the seven prints X, cut 13 squares 2⅞in/7.3cm.

6 From print E, cut 13 tree trunks 1¼ x 4½in/3.1 x 11.4cm.

7 For the fill in triangles, cut two squares from F, 15⅜in/38.1cm. Cut each across the diagonals to yield eight triangles. Cut two 8in/20.3cm squares for the corners. Cut across the diagonal to make four triangles.

8 For the inner border, from the orange floral print (G), cut four strips 2in/5cm wide x the fabric width.

9 For the middle border, using the black leaf-on-cream ground print (H), cut four lengths 5in/12.7cm wide across the width of the fabric.

10 For the outer sawtooth border, from the black leaf-on-cream ground print cut 42 squares each 3⅞in/9.8cm. Cut the same from the collective seven mixed print X designs.

11 For binding, cut sufficient strips 1½in/3.8cm wide across the width of the fabric to total 256in/6.5m when joined together.

SEWING
Make 13 Tree of Life blocks.
Finished size of each block
10½ x 10½in/26.7 x 26.7cm

1 Study fig 1 to understand the placement of each unit. To make 14 bi-colored squares for each tree you need four squares 2⅞in/7.3cm of print A, three of print B, and seven from the mixed prints X, one from each design.

2 Pair up the blocks to make rows comprising A and X, and B and X. On the reverse of the lightest fabric, draw a line across the diagonal.

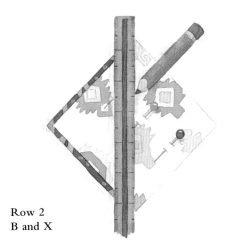

Row 2
B and X

3 Pin pairs right sides together. Sew ¼in/6mm to each side of the line.

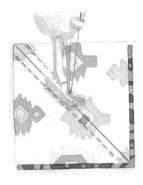

Row 2
B and X

4 Cut between the two stitched lines on the pencil line. Repeat, to make eight pieced squares using fabrics A and X, and six pieced squares using B and X for each of the 13 blocks.

5 For each block you will need three half-square triangles. Cut each of the 20 print D squares across the diagonal. Discard one triangle and distribute the remaining 39 among the 13 blocks.

6 With the 14 bi-colored squares, the five remaining 2½in/6.4cm squares (A x 1; B x 1; C x 3), and the three triangles from print D, make up 13 Tree of Life blocks.

7 To complete the block, cut the 6½in/16.5cm square in half across the diagonal. Place the tree trunk between the two half triangles.

8 Stitch the three pieces together.

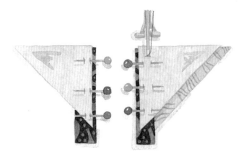

9 Trim the end of the tree trunk so that it aligns with the right angle shape of the triangle. Stitch the tree trunk to the top half of the tree. Make twelve more blocks.

10 Use the photograph below right as a guide to placing each Tree of Life block, corner and fill in block. Assemble the blocks in diagonal rows beginning with the top left block. Add two fill in triangles to each side. For row 2, stitch together three blocks and two fill in triangles. For row three, stitch together five blocks and two corner triangles. Continue piecing the blocks and fill in triangles.

11 Stitch the five diagonal rows together, beginning by adding a corner to the top left-hand block. Add the last corner to the bottom right-hand corner.

12 Center the orange border (F), on each side of the quilt panel. Stitch each border to each edge to within ¼in/6mm of each corner. Miter each corner. *(see page 137 of the Techniques and Templates chapter)*

13 Attach the black leaf-on-cream border (H), as for step 12.

14 Follow steps 2–4 to make up 84 bi-colored squares for the sawtooth border, with one half using the black leaf-on-cream print.

15 Stitch together two rows of 20 bi-colored squares and two rows of 22 bi-colored squares, ensuring that each black leaf-on-cream print is in the same direction on each row.

16 Stitch each shorter border to the sides of the quilt. Ensure the mixed prints (X) are on the outer edge. Sew the long borders across the quilt top and bottom.

17 Make and attach continuous binding. *(see pages 137 and 138)*

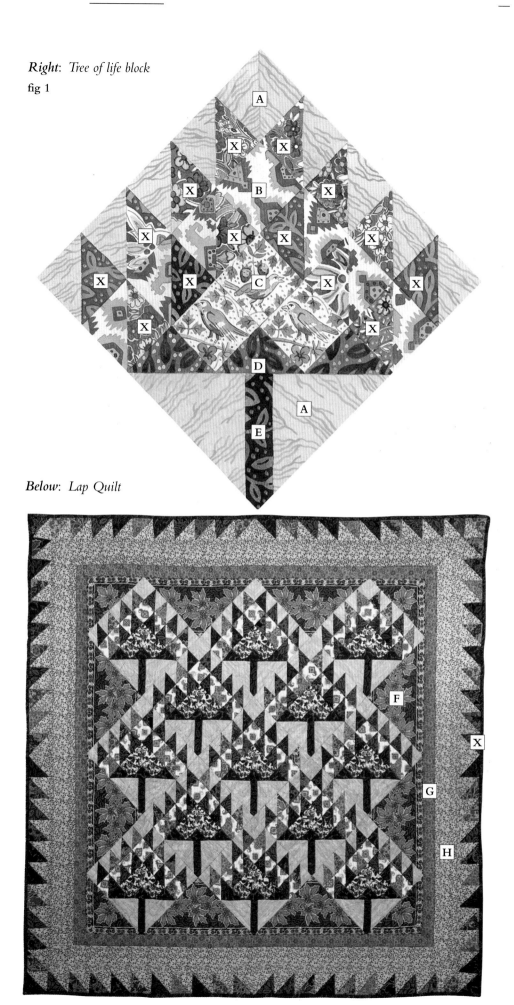

Right: *Tree of life block*

fig 1

Below: *Lap Quilt*

Appliqué Lampshade

MATERIALS

- Plain-color purchased lampshade
- Royal blue to bind the top and bottom of the lampshade
- One red *Briarwood* cushion panel
- One blue *Briarwood* cushion panel
- Fine white cotton to back the motifs ~ ¼ yd/25cm
- Fusible web ~ ¼ yd/25cm
- Fabric adhesive

CUTTING

1 For the binding, measure the circumference of the top and bottom of the lampshade and add 2in/5cm to each measurement.

2 Cut strips 1¾in/4.5cm wide x the length of your measurements. Fold in half lengthways and press. Fold the raw edges in to the center foldline on each long edge. Press.

3 Determine which motifs from the red and blue cushion panels are required. Rough cut slightly larger shapes from white cotton.

4 Following the manufacturer's instructions, iron fusible web to the reverse of each motif. Remove the paper backing, then fuse the white cotton to the web. Accurately cut out each motif, following the printed black lines of the design.

MAKING

1 Prepare the bottom of the lampshade for binding by applying fabric adhesive to the baseline of the lampshade. Open out the center fold of the binding. Beginning at the bottom edge of the lampshade with the seam facing you, align the center foldline of the wrong side of the binding with the bottom glued edge of the lampshade. Apply the top half of the binding to the glued area stretching slightly to fit.

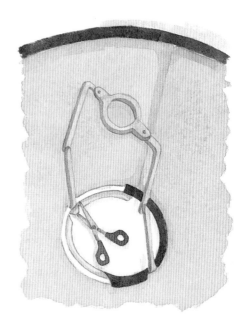

2 Trim the short end of the binding so that there is a ¾in/1.9cm overlap. Turn under ½in/1.3cm on the overlapping raw edge and stick in place.

3 Turn the binding in to the inside of the lampshade and repeat.

4 Repeat at the top edge. Where the binding crosses any part of the wire frame, clip and trim the binding with very sharp scissors.

5 Decorate half of the shade with red motifs and half with blue motifs. Apply fabric adhesive to the white cotton backing of the motifs. Allow to dry slightly then stick in place on the shade. Have a cloth available to wipe away any excess adhesive.

Patchwork Drape

*Finished size 54 x 72in/
137.2 x 182.8cm*

MATERIALS

*Adapt the materials to your own
requirements ~ allow 8in/20.3cm
longer than the finished length for top
and bottom hems and 6in/15.2cm
wider than the finished width for the
two side hems.*

- Blue for the drape ~ 2½yd/
  2.3m of 60in/152cm wide
  herringbone weave
- Lining ~ 2yd/1.8m of
  60in/152cm wide fabric
- Braid ~ 3⅓yd/3.1m
- Eight rectangles in different
  prints each 7 x 10in/17.8 x
  25.4cm for the top patchwork
  decoration
- 13 rectangles 7 x 8½in/17.8 x
  21.6cm for the side patchwork
- One piece 8½ x 10in/21.6 x
  25.4cm for the top corner
  patch
- Two round weights for the
  bottom of the drape
- Drape pole with rings
- Finial
- Pincer clips for hanging

CUTTING

1 For the drape, from blue, cut one
piece 80 x 58in/203.2 x 147.3cm.
For the top of the lining, cut one
piece 7in/17.8cm across the width of
the fabric.

2 For the lining, cut one piece 70 x
55in/178 x 139.7cm.

SEWING

- Use ½in/1.3cm seams throughout.

Patchwork

1 Patchwork side—With right sides
together, pin and sew the 7 x 8½in/
17.8 x 26.7cm pieces together along
the 8½in/21.6cm edge. (The last
rectangle will be turned in and form
part of the hemline). Alternate the
prints. Press the seams open.

2 Patchwork top—Sew together the
eight pieces along the 10in/25.4cm
edge. Press the seams open.

3 With right sides together, stitch the
corner to the left-hand end of the top.

4 With right sides together and raw
edges aligned, sew the top to the
patchwork side.

5 Press the inside seam allowances to
the wrong side.

6 Position the wrong side of the
patchwork to the right side of the
drape, raw edges aligned with the raw
edges of the top and side drape. Pin.
Machine topstitch the inside edge of
the patchwork in place. Baste the
outside raw edges to the drape.

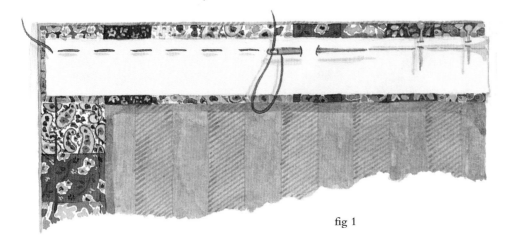

fig 1

Drape

1 Turn in 2in/5cm at the top and press. Turn in 3in/7.6cm at the bottom. Press. Turn in another 3in/7.6cm and press. Open all folds.

2 With right sides together, align the raw edge of the 7in/17.8cm blue strip with the top edge of the drape. Slide the strip down so that it sits 1½in/3.8cm below the raw edge.

3 Baste and sew across the top only using the 2in/5cm foldline as the stitching line. Press. *(see fig 1)*

4 Turn in 2in/5cm at each side of the drape and press. Open out the folds.

5 Miter the two bottom corners. Turn in the first fold at the bottom edge. Fold the corners in to the point where the pressed foldlines cross. Trim

off the points. Press. Refold each side seam and the bottom edge. Hand stitch the miter.

6 Make small pockets from fabric scraps to wrap the weights in. Stitch around the raw edges of the pocket and stitch inside the miter.

7 Stitch the hemlines in place.

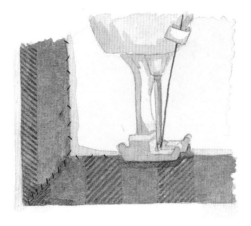

Lining

1 Turn in 2in/5cm at the bottom and press. Turn in another 2in/5cm and press. Open out the folds.

2 Turn in 1½in/3.8cm at each side and press. Refold the hemline and stitch the seam.

3 Spread out the drape right side down. On top, right side up, position the lining 1in/2.5cm from the folded sides and bottom of the drape. Pin and

slipstitch in position to the two sides only.

4 Turn in ½in/1.3cm of the blue strip at the top of the drape and press.

5 Fold the strip over the lining so that the seam joining it to the patchwork is at the top of the drape and the turned in raw edge covers the raw edge at the top of the lining. Press and topstitch in place.

Finishing

1 Add the braid to the seam joining the patchwork to the drape. Turn in 1in/2.5cm at one end. Beginning at the bottom of the drape, pin the braid in place.

2 At the corner, make a mock miter and continue pinning to the right-hand side of the drape. Trim 1in/2.5cm longer than required and turn in the raw edge. Stitch in place.

3 To hang the drape, attach pincer clips to the top. The clips should be spaced quite close together to support the weight of the fabric.

Fabric Picture Mounts

MATERIALS

- Mount board to make the mount
- Cutting mat, metal ruler, pencil, art knife, sewing scissors
- Double-sided adhesive tape or PVA glue
- Sufficient fabric to cover the size of the mount
- Round-headed pins
- Fray-checking solution
- Batting (optional)

COVERING RECTANGLES OR SQUARES

1 Decide on the outer dimensions of the mount: this may be predetermined by the size of your picture frame. On mount board, using a pencil and ruler, draw the finished outer size, ensuring that the corners are true 90° right angles. Cut out using a metal ruler and art knife.

2 Decide on the height and width of the window area: this will be determined by the dimensions of the picture to be framed, and the border area required around the picture.

3 Draw the dimensions of the window on the mount, equal distances from each side so that the framing area is centered.

4 Cut fabric larger than the size of the mount board. Add on to each side half of the width of the mount.

5 Pin the fabric along the edges of the mount, pulling the fabric taut but

not distorting the fabric pattern. Fold in the excess fabric at the corners.

6 Apply PVA glue or double-sided adhesive tape to the raw edges of the fabric.

7 Turn in the top and bottom first. Press flat with your thumb. If gluing allow the adhesive to dry, then remove the holding pins.

8 Cut out the window area allowing half of the width of the mount to turn back and glue.

9 With sewing scissors clip into the corners at a 45° angle. A spot of fray-checking solution at the corners before clipping will ensure that the clip is not visible from the front.

10 Apply glue or double-sided adhesive tape to the raw edges as before and turn back the fabric over the mount.

COVERING OVAL MOUNTS

MATERIALS

- **Mount board to make the mount**
- **Cutting mat, metal ruler, pencil, art knife, sewing scissors**
- **Double-sided adhesive tape or PVA glue**
- **Sufficient fabric to cover the size of the mount**
- **Round-headed pins**
- **Fray-checking solution**
- **Batting (optional)**

1 Cut the dimensions of the mount from mount board as in step 1 for Covering Rectangles or Squares on page 89.

2 Decide on the height and width of the oval window.

3 Draw horizontal and vertical lines through the point where the center of the oval window will be positioned.

4 Mark the height and width of the window on the drawn lines and mark the horizontal point X and the vertical X. *(see pic at top of column 2)*

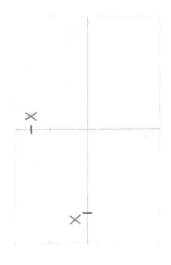

5 Place a strip of card on the horizontal line. At one end mark the center point A where the two lines cross. Keep A at the center and mark X on the card. Move the card so that X is aligned with the vertical point X.

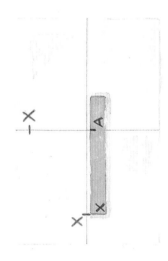

6 Mark a second point where the center lines cross, label this point B.

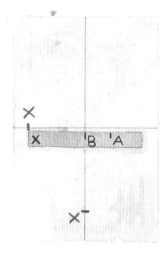

7 Rotate the strip in one direction, ensuring that A remains on the vertical line and B remains on the horizontal line.

8 At the opposite end mark a dot on the mount board at regular intervals around the ellipse. The more dots there are the more accurate the ellipse is likely to be.

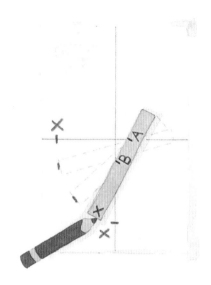

9 When you return to the beginning, join up the dots. Carefully and accurately cut out the oval.

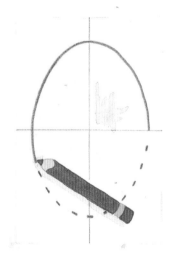

10 Follow steps 4 and 10 above in Covering Rectangles or Squares to cover the mount. Allow extra fabric if you choose to use batting and make the mount padded.

11 If desired, cut the batting slightly smaller than the outer dimensions of the mount. Then cut the window slightly larger.

12 Cut out the window area allowing extra fabric to fold back and glue. Use fray-checking solution on the area to be clipped.

13 Using sewing scissors, clip around the extra allowance at a 90° angle, but do not clip right up to the mount board. Clip at regular intervals to ease turning the fabric around the curved area.

14 Glue the raw edges. Fold the fabric back, pulling tightly.

Right: *Oval shaped fabric mount hung from green velvet ribbon.*

Nursery

The Voysey collection, used to furnish the Nursery is an adaptation of the original fabric—The House That Jack Built—designed by Charles Francis Voysey in 1929. Like William Morris, Voysey was an architect by training, who designed wallpaper and fabric patterns between commissions. His early work from the 1880s is distinctive, portraying stylized repeat floral patterns. By the turn of the century his work had developed to illustrate a narrative theme such as The House That Jack Built, most of which was designed to be used in the nursery. To make the original design more popular, the disproportionate-size rats (as large as the house) were left out when printed by Morton Sundour.

NVT
TREE

DA
TLE

A

B

7

8

9

10

1

3

6

~ Pinboard for the Nursery ~

The pinboard displays the main sources of inspiration for the blinds, quilt and soft toys for the Nursery.

This is the cow with the crumpled horn,
that tossed the dog, that worried the cat,
that killed the rat, that ate the malt
that lay in the house that Jack built.

The fabric collection, based on the nursery rhyme provided the direction for the projects. The animal motifs inspired in turn delightful stencils for decorating walls and furniture.

No child's room is complete without the marvellous illustrations of Walter Crane executed for the *Baby Opera* (*see A and B*). This book proved to be a best-seller at Liberty's after its publication.

....

1 Open floral design from the *Voysey* collection

2 Yellow check

3 Solid yellow for the blind border

4 Small berry design

5 Patchwork motif design from the *Voysey* collection

6 All-over rambling vine design from the *Voysey* collection

7 Illustrations from Walter Crane's *Baby Opera*,
A *Mary, Mary Quite Contrary*
B *I had a Little Nut Tree*

8 Ribbon Work

9 Embroidery

10 Stencils

11 Tana lawn *(Capel)*

....

Checkered Roman Blind

*Finished size 42 x 52in/
106.7 x 132cm*

MATERIALS

*Read the Materials list, then adapt the
measurements to suit your own
requirements.*

- **Roman blind kit to include
  rings, rods, Stick & Sew strip,
  cords, cleat, batten, eyelets and
  assembly instructions in a
  suitable size**
- **Yellow check for the blind ~
  1¾yd/1.6m of 60in/152cm
  wide fabric**
- **Solid yellow for the decoration
  ~ ½yd/40cm of 60in/152cm
  wide fabric**
- **Scraps of red, and green for the
  motifs**
- **Red, and green ⅛in/3mm
  wide ribbon ~ 2yd/2m of each
  color**
- **Scraps of fusible web**
- **Backing ~ 1½yd/1.4m of
  60in/152cm wide fabric**

CUTTING

1 From yellow check, cut one piece
47 x 46in/119.4 x 116.8cm.

2 From solid yellow, for the lower
part of the blind, cut one piece 47 x
13in/119.4 x 33cm.

3 Bond and cut ten flowers and
leaves from appropriate fabric scraps.

4 For backing, cut one piece 45 x
55in/114.3 x 139.7cm. From the
remainder, cut two pockets for the
dowels 2½ x 43in/6.4 x 109.2cm.

SEWING

- Use a ½in/1.3cm seam allowance
unless otherwise stated.

1 On one long edge of yellow, turn
in 3in/7.6cm to the wrong side and
press. Open out the fold.

2 Arrange each of the motifs on the
right side of the yellow ½in/1.3cm
above the folded edge and
2½in/6.4cm in from each short edge.
The top of the flower circle should be
1½in/3.8cm below the remaining long
edge.

3 When you are happy with the
arrangement, remove the paper
backing from the fusible web and
bond each in position.

4 Satin stitch each motif using
appropriate color thread.

5 With green ribbon and using long
running stitch embroider the curved
stems of the flowers.

6 With red ribbon, stab stitch around
the outer edges of the flower heads.

7 With right sides together and
flower head uppermost, align the long
raw edge of yellow with the 47in/
119.4cm raw edge of yellow check.

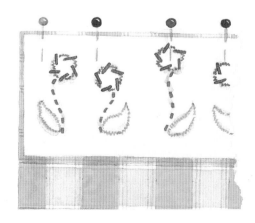

8 Sew together using a ½in/1.3cm seam and press the seam toward the solid yellow.

9 Turn in ½in/1.3m at the two sides and press. Turn in another 2in/5cm and press.

10 At the bottom turn in ½in/1.3cm and press. Turn in another 2½in/ 6.4cm along this edge and press all turnings with a damp cloth. Open out the fold at the bottom edge. Leave the top edge raw.

11 Prepare the backing by turning in 1½in/3.8cm on each side and lower edge. Press with a damp cloth. Leave the top edge raw.

12 With wrong sides together, and aligning top raw edges, center the backing on the blind. Pin in place.

13 Slipstitch the backing to the turned in seam allowance of the yellow and yellow check at the two sides only.

14 Machine stitch across the top raw edges to hold the blind and lining together and overcast the raw edges.

15 Refold the yellow at the bottom edge encasing the backing. Slide a rod into the fold. Pin.

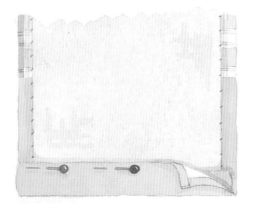

16 Slipstitch the folded edge of yellow to the backing.

17 Turning in ¼in/6mm along each long edge of the two pockets. Press. Fold the lengths in half wrong sides together. Press. Sew along the long edge and one short edge.

18 On the backing, mark with pins the position of the first pocket 17in/43.2cm from the lower edge. Mark the second pocket position 17in/43.2cm from the first pocket. Center one long edge of one pocket on the marked line and baste in place through all layers of the blind. Sew along the long edge. Repeat with the second pocket.

19 Slide a rod into each pocket, then slipstitch the short edge closed.

20 Stitch on one ring 1in/2.5cm from each end of the pocket on the pressed line. Stitch two more rings across the pocket, spacing the rings evenly from each end.

21 At the top of the blind, turn the raw edges in using 1in/2.5cm seam.

22 Align the "sew" side of the Stick & Sew strip with the top of the wrong side of the blind. Pin and stitch in position along each edge.

23 Refer to the manufacturer's instructions to insert the cords in the blind and to attach the batten and eyelets to the blind.

Right: Detail of flower appliqué with ribbon stitching for the flower stem and large stab stitches around the flower face.

Soft Tumbling Blocks

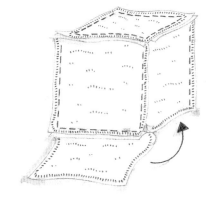

Finished size **4in/10.2cm cube**

MATERIALS

- **Fabric scraps ~ six squares 5in/13cm**
- **Light-weight batting ~ six squares 5in/13cm**
- **One foam cube 3¾in/9.5cm**

CUTTING

From fabric scraps, cut six squares 4½ x 4½in/11.4 x 11.4cm. Cut the same from batting.

SEWING

- ¼in/6mm seam allowance has been used throughout.

1 Baste each batting square to the reverse of each fabric square, raw edges level.

2 Machine or hand quilt around the outline of any predominant motifs as desired.

3 Arrange four squares in a row as in fig 1 below.

4 With right sides together, sew the squares together beginning ¼in/6mm from the raw edge and ending ¼in/6mm from the raw edge. Treat the batting and fabric as one piece.

5 Sew together the two free edges to make a cube shape (*see fig 2 below*).

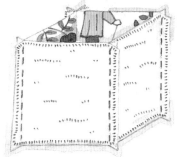

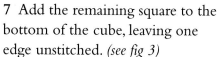

fig 2

6 With batting side out, pin and sew another square to the cube top.

7 Add the remaining square to the bottom of the cube, leaving one edge unstitched. (*see fig 3*)

8 Turn the fabric cube right side out. Insert the foam cube.

9 Slipstitch the free edge closed.

fig 3

fig 1

Cot Quilt

*Finished size 36 x 60in/
91.4 x 152.4cm*

MATERIALS

- Fabric A animal motif print for the centers of the picture blocks ~ ¾yd/70cm
- Fabric B for the tulip blocks and picture blocks ~ 1½yd/1.4m
- Fabric C berry print for the sashing strips ~ ¾ yd/70cm
- Fabric D floral print for the borders ~ ¾yd/70cm
- Mustard ~ ¾yd/70cm
- Blue ~ ½yd/50cm
- Backing ~ 1¾yd/1.6m
- Batting ~ 1¾yd/1.6m

CUTTING

1 From fabric A, for the picture blocks cut nine squares 5½ x 5½in/ 14 x 14cm, and four squares 4¼ x 4¼in/10.8 x 10.8cm.

2 From fabric B, for the picture blocks, cut nine squares each 5½ x 5½in/14 x 14cm. Cut 28 squares each 2½ x 2½in/6.4 x 6.4cm centering the tulip on each square.

3 From fabric C cut nine strips 2½ x 44in/6.4 x 111.8cm for the sashing strips.

4 From blue, to frame the picture blocks, cut twelve lengths 1 x 44in/2.5 x 111.8cm.

5 From mustard, to frame the picture blocks cut twelve lengths ¾ x 44in/1.9 x 111.8cm. For the border trim, cut five strips from mustard 1½ x 44in/3.8 x 111.8cm. For the binding, cut five strips 2¼ x 44in/6.4 x 111.8cm.

6 From fabric D, for the borders cut five strips 4¼ x 44in/10.8 x 111.8cm.

SEWING

1 To frame the 5½in/14cm picture blocks, sew blue lengths to right and left-hand sides. Press and trim.

2 Stitch blue lengths across top and bottom. Press and trim.

3 Repeat using the ¾in/1.9cm wide mustard lengths, stitching the strips to each side, then top and bottom.

4 Arrange the 18 blocks into six rows of three, alternating the patterned blocks horizontally and vertically.

5 Add the sashing strips to the left-hand side of each block. Align the raw edges of the sashing with the mustard framing strips. Pin, then stitch together. Trim the sashing level with the top and bottom of the block at a true right angle. Press. Add another strip of sashing to the right-hand side of the right-hand blocks. Trim. Press toward the sashing.

6 Join the three blocks together to make one length 28 x 7in/71.1 x 17.8cm. Press.

7 With right sides together, stitch one tulip square to the left-hand short end of a sashing strip. Pin the strip along the top edge of one block, matching the seam of the tulip square with the vertical sashing seam. Sew across the top of the first block to within ¾in/1.9cm of the next sashing seam.

8 Fold the horizontal sashing back on itself and fingerpress to mark the seam line. Unfold the sashing and trim ¼in/6mm beyond the foldline.

9 Add the second tulip square, then rejoin the sashing to the other side. Continue across the top to finish with a tulip square.

10 Repeat along the top edge of the remaining lengths. Add another length of horizontal sashing to the bottom edge of the last block. Press carefully.

11 With right sides together, stitch the six strips together to make one panel, aligning all seams. Press.

12 Mustard border trim for the top and bottom—Fold two lengths 1½in/3.8cm wide in half lengthways, wrong sides together. Press. With raw edges aligned, and the folded edge toward the quilt, baste in position.

13 On top of the mustard trim, baste one fabric D border, right side down. Trim the excess mustard and border D level with the sides of the quilt center. Stitch through all the layers. Remove the basting. Press the border outward and trim. Put the surplus mustard on one side to use at step 16.

14 Trim for each vertical side of the quilt—With right sides together stitch the three remaining 1½in/3.8cm mustard strips to make one continuous length. Cut into two. Fold in half lengthways wrong sides together and press. With raw edges aligned, baste and stitch to the sides of the quilt. Trim the excess.

15 Stitch together the three fabric D lengths at the short end. Press seams open. Fold and cut the strip in half to yield two 66in/167.6cm lengths.

16 To the lower end of the border, baste a folded piece of mustard trim left over from step 13. Trim to size. Over the mustard, right side down, place a 4¼in/10.8cm square of fabric A, ensuring the design runs in the correct direction. Stitch through all layers. Press the folded edge of the trim toward the picture square.

17 Baste the border along the left-hand side of the quilt, starting at the bottom left-hand side and aligning seams. Stitch to within 6in/15.2cm of the top of the quilt. Fold the border back on itself at the point where the berry and tulip sashing meet the border. Fingerpress the fold down. Unfold the border and trim ¼in/6mm beyond this point.

18 Baste another piece of mustard trim and a second 4¼in/10.8cm square to the top edge of the border. Stitch in position.

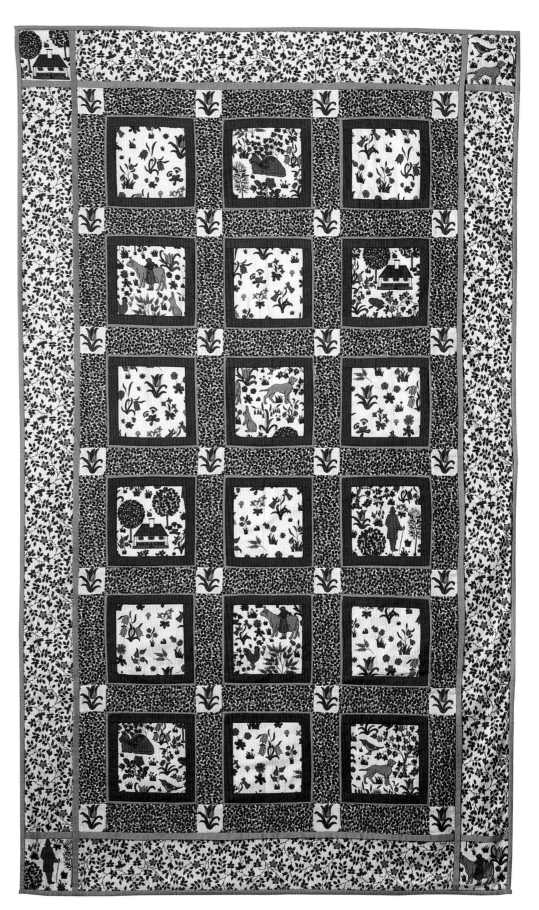

19 Trim all edges even. Press. Repeat at the right-hand side of the quilt, working from the top to bottom.

20 Make up the quilt sandwich. *(see page 138)* Hand or machine quilt as desired. Bind the quilt. *(see page 138)*

THE
JA

~ Pinboard for the Nursery ~

The pinboard opposite displays some of the illustrations considered in designing the projects for the nursery.

Illustrator of children's books, Kate Greenaway had a tremendous impact on the design of children's clothes sold by Liberty. Arthur Lasenby greatly admired her style, and dresses in the style of Kate Greenaway appeared in the 1887 catalog *Artistic Dress for Children*. Isadora Duncan describes a dress she bought for herself from the children's department in Liberty's—"*A white muslin Kate Greenaway dress, with a blue sash under the arms and big straw hat on my head, and my hair in curls on my shoulders.*"

....

1 Panel print from the *Voysey* collection

2 Rambling vine design from the *Voysey* collection

3 All-over design from the *Voysey* collection

4 Kate Greenaway nursery illustrations

5 Nursery rhymes

6 Postcards of tiles designed by William Morris and Ford Madox Brown

7 Stuffed toy birds for the wallhanging

8 Prairie points

9 Designs for animal toys

....

Jack's Wallhanging

Finished size 27 x 36in/
68.6 x 91.5cm

MATERIALS

- **One pre-printed House That Jack Built panel**
- **Blue for the borders ~ ¼yd/30cm**
- **Yellow for the binding ~ ¼yd/30cm**
- **Red for the prairie point edging ~ ¼yd/30cm**
- **Backing (includes sufficient to make a hanging sleeve) ~ 1yd/1m**
- **Stiff fusible interfacing ~ 1yd/1m**
- **Fabric scraps for the birds**
- **Small amount of toy filling**
- **Assorted beads**
- **Six-stranded embroidery floss**
- **Dowel ~ 1yd/1m**

CUTTING

1 Cut the panel 28 x 37in/71.1 x 93.9cm.

2 Cut four yellow strips 1¾in/4.5cm wide x the width of the fabric.

3 Cut four blue binding strips 1½in/3.8cm wide x the fabric width.

4 From red, cut two lengths 3in/ 7.6cm wide x the width of the fabric.

5 Make patterns for the birds on page 143. Cut seven right- and seven left-facing bodies. Bond and cut 14 wings and eyes. Cut 14 legs, 28 feet and seven beaks.

6 Cut a hanging sleeve 3 x 25in/7.6 x 63.5cm.

SEWING

- Use ½in/1.3cm seams throughout.

1 To the sides of the panel, with right sides together and raw edges aligned, stitch the yellow border strips. Trim to size. Press the seams toward the border. Stitch the borders to the top and bottom. Trim to size and press.

2 Fuse interfacing to the wrong side of the panel. On top of the interfacing pin the backing, right side up. Baste. Trim all raw edges level.

3 Fold the binding in half lengthways and press. Open out the folds. With right sides together and raw edges aligned, pin and stitch the binding to the sides of the quilt. Trim to size. Fold the binding over the stitching line to the back of the quilt. Turn in the raw edge and slipstitch in place. Repeat at the top and bottom, trimming the binding to 1in/2.5cm longer than required and turning in a ½in/1.3cm seam at the short ends.

4 Baste the two lengths of red right sides together. On the wrong side of one length of red, draw the prairie point zigzag ¼in/6mm from the raw edge. Sew along the zigzag. One stitch across the point makes a neat point when turned right side out.

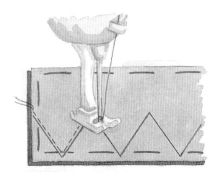

5 Trim the excess away from the stitching, clipping close to the stitched line. Turn right side out and gently ease out the points. Press. Overcast the remaining long raw edge.

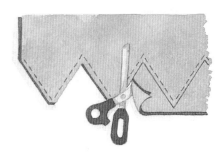

6 Trim the border ½in/1.3cm longer than the wallhanging' width. Turn in ¼in/6mm at the short ends and the remaining long end. Press and stitch. Pin in place.

7 Overstitch the seam line attaching the binding to the border.

8 Stitch beads to the edging as desired.

Birds

1 Bond the wings and eyes. Add a bead for the pupil.

2 Legs—Turn in a small seam along each edge. Fold in half aligning folded edges. Slipstitch the seam.

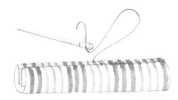

3 Feet—Turn in a small seam on each and slipstitch two together, leaving the top edge free to slip a leg into. Attach a leg to a foot.

4 Place a right and left-facing body right sides together. Place the legs inside the body. Align the unstitched end with the raw edge of the underside of the body. Stitch the body leaving a small opening under the tail. Turn the body out through the gap and stuff with toy filling. Slipstitch.

5 Beak—Snip into the center of the circle. Overlap to form a cone. Sew. Stuff the beak. Slipstitch to the body.

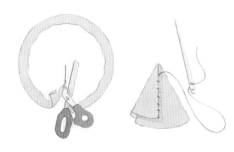

6 Thread each bird on a length of cotton. Stitch through the center bird back. Thread beads onto the length. Stitch to the edging and knot.

Right: *Birds from the Wallhanging trim.*

Dressing Room

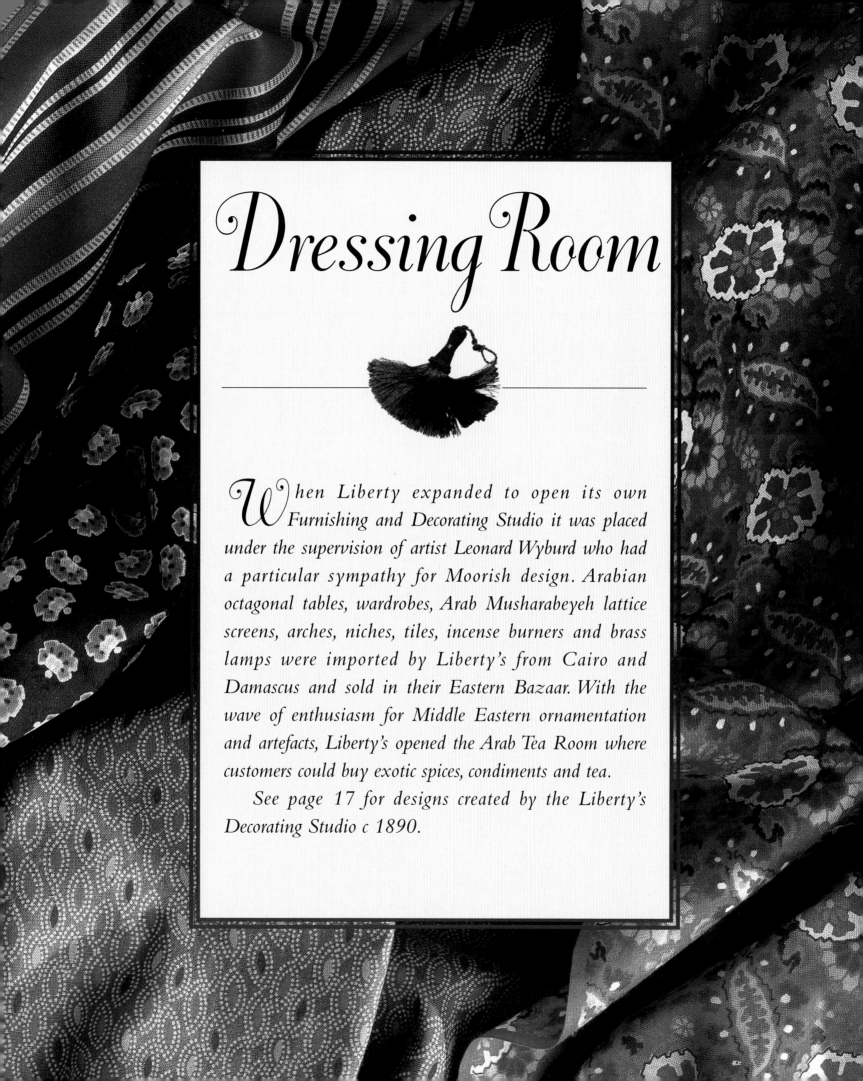

When Liberty expanded to open its own Furnishing and Decorating Studio it was placed under the supervision of artist Leonard Wyburd who had a particular sympathy for Moorish design. Arabian octagonal tables, wardrobes, Arab Musharabeyeh lattice screens, arches, niches, tiles, incense burners and brass lamps were imported by Liberty's from Cairo and Damascus and sold in their Eastern Bazaar. With the wave of enthusiasm for Middle Eastern ornamentation and artefacts, Liberty's opened the Arab Tea Room where customers could buy exotic spices, condiments and tea.

See page 17 for designs created by the Liberty's Decorating Studio c 1890.

~ Pinboard for the Dressing Room ~

I found a description of a boudoir in one of Liberty's old interiors' catalog and it prompted the inclusion of this luxury room in the book.

"The Boudoir, which is the 'Bower' of the olden time, being the room especially appertaining to the Mistress of the House should be decorated light and elegant rather than in a formal manner. Here if anywhere severe rule may be relaxed in favour of dainty refinement and grace, soft draperies, brightly coloured cushions and knick-knacks of various kinds may not inaptly find a place in the boudoir, which an exacting judgement might banish from the more prosaic rooms of the house."

Furnished "Arabic style," the projects in this chapter offer a wonderful and quite practical solution for problems of storage—tents, bags, and boxes—colorful and portable—just like a Bedouin's caravan.

....

1 *Napier* fabric collection in red colorway

2 Red berries design *(Tree of Life collection)*

3 Tana lawn *(Ianthe)*

4 Wardrobe structure

5 Tassels and braids

6 Fret work

....

Moorish Wardrobe Tent

Finished size 19½ deep x 35 wide x 70½in high (97in high to the top of the finial) / 49.5 x 88.9 x 179.1cm (246cm high to the top of the finial)

MATERIALS

FOR THE WARDROBE FRAME

Read the instructions before buying any materials and adapt the measurements to your own requirements.

- Two shelving units for the sides of the wardrobe ~ 70½ x 19½in/179.1 x 49.5cm
- Four shelves ~ 33 x 19½ x 1in/83.8 x 49.5 x 2.5cm
- Eight 2in/5cm long metal rods to fit into the shelving units and support the shelves
- One brace and four screws to hold it in place
- One round disc 1in/2.5cm thick and screws to hold it in place
- One length of dowel 1in/2.5cm thick x 18in/45cm
- One cardboard or plastic tube for the apex of the tent ~ 2½in/6.4cm in diameter x 18in/45cm long
- One finial
- Paint for the frame and shelves
- Wire to carry the drapes on
- Two metal eyelets to fix the wire to the frame
- One metal hook to hold the center of the wire between the two drapes

ASSEMBLING THE WARDROBE FRAME
(see diagram on page 114)

Shelves

1 Hold the shelving units parallel to each other, with the rungs horizontal.

2 Decide on the position of the shelves—use one to form the top of the wardrobe, and a second for the base—this allows for hanging space. If you wish, add as many shelves as suits your needs.

3 Insert the metal rods into the holes in the inside edge of the shelving units, parallel to each other and in the desired position.

4 To fit the shelves to the frame, each of the corners needs to be cut away. We made a cut ½in/1.3cm wide and 1½in/3.8cm long.

5 The shelves should rest securely on the metal rods and should fit neatly to the frame. The shelves should fit snugly, but not so tightly that they cannot be removed. If they are too tight, use sandpaper to adjust the fit.

Frame

To support the frame a brace holds the shelving units apart at the lower half of the wardrobe back. It is screwed into the depth of the frame at each side. The angle of the cross needs to be set as near to 90° to provide most stability. *(see drawing on page 114)*

Canopy

1 The wooden disc which supports the apex of the tent, has a 1in/2.5cm circle cut into its center point. The circle should be large enough to slot the 1in/2.5cm diameter wooden dowel into and to hold it securely.

2 The center of the disc is screwed to the center top of the top shelf.

3 The dowel is fitted into the cut away center of the disc—use glue to secure the position.

4 The cardboard tube should slot over the top of the dowel. The base of the finial will eventually be glued to the other end of the dowel and rest on the cardboard tube.

5 The gathered fabric at the top of the canopy will tuck into the tube.

6 The assembled unit fits on the top of the top shelf of the wardrobe.

Drapes

1 Attach two metal hooks to each side of the front of the frame just below the top shelf.

2 Screw a metal hook into the underside of the top shelf at the front.

3 The drape wire should fit over the hooks at each side and rest on the hook in the center front. It should stretch slightly to fit so that it holds the drapes taut across the front of the tent.

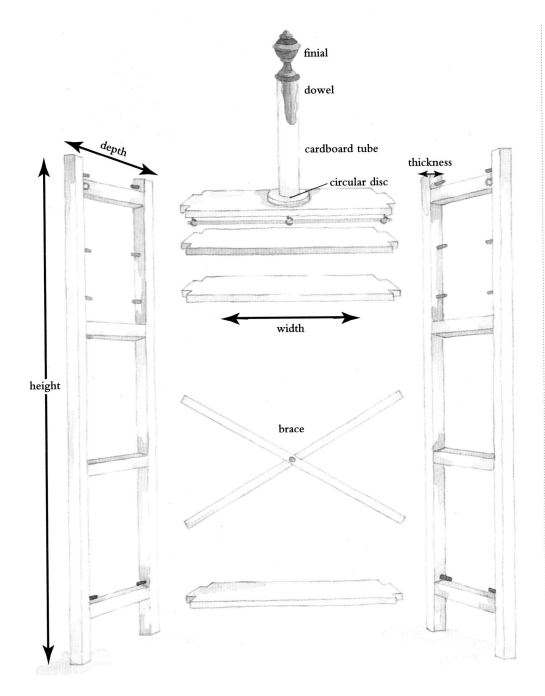

finial

dowel

cardboard tube

circular disc

depth

thickness

width

height

brace

MEASURING AND CUTTING
Wardrobe tent

1 To determine the length of striped fabric required, measure the height of the shelving unit and add to this measurement 1in/2.5cm for turnings.

2 To determine the number of fabric widths required, measure the width of the frame. Add to this measurement the depth of the frame twice + 12in/30.5cm for the wrap around fronts of the frame + 1in/2.5cm for turnings. Divide the measurement by the width of the fabric you will use: for example a frame with a width of 35in/88.9cm and a depth of 19½in/49.5cm will require 87in/221cm of fabric: (35 + 19½ + 19½ + 12 +1 = 87in/88.9 + 49.5 + 49.5 + 30.5 + 2.5 = 220.9cm). The calculation requires two widths of fabric based on a fabric width of 45in/114.3cm.

3 Calculate the same amount for the berry lining.

4 Striped fabric to cover the bottom shelf—Measure the shelf and add to the depth the drop from the bottom shelf to the ground. Add ½in/1.3cm on all sides for turning under.

Canopy

1 Measure in a diagonal from the top of the frame to the apex, just below the finial. Add to your measurement 7½in/19cm for the scallop + 5in/12.7cm to allow for turnings.

2 To determine the number of widths required, measure the circumference of the wardrobe frame and add to your measurement 6in/15.2cm for overlap and turnings. Divide the total by the width of your chosen fabric.

MATERIALS
FOR THE FABRIC CASING AND CANOPY

- Blue and red stripe fabric for the canopy, wardrobe, and shelf
- Braid for the shelf edging and the scallop of the canopy
- Red berry fabric for the drapes and lining
- Solid red for binding the bottom of the wardrobe casing
- Stapler
- Plastic lengths to weight the

bottom of the tent ~ 1in/2.5cm wide x ⅛in/3mm thick, two at 6in/15cm long, two 19in/48cm long, and one 35in/89cm long
- Velcro
- Fusible pelmet Vilene with Velcro-like loops
- Glue to attach Velcro to the frame
- Four weights for the bottom of the drapes

Berry drapes

1 Allow one fabric width for each half of the pair. For the length, measure the height of the wardrobe and add to your measurement 2in/5cm for turnings and the wire casing at the drape top.

2 Red binding to encase the weights at the bottom—Cut 4in/10.2cm wide strips, one piece the width of the back, two pieces the depth of the frame, and two pieces for the wrap around front 7in/17.8cm long.

3 For the pelmet Vilene to make the scalloped edge of the canopy, measure the circumference of the wardrobe frame and add 3in/7.6cm. Cut one piece the length of your measurement x 7½in/19cm wide.

4 Calculate the amount of braid needed at steps 7 and 9 of the Canopy instructions on page 117.

Velcro

To calculate the amount of Velcro, measure the circumference of the frame, and double the measurement. This will give sufficient to attach the wardrobe casing to the frame, the canopy to the top of the casing, and leave sufficient to attach to the bottom of the wrap around of the canopy. Cut the length in half, trim the other lengths later.

SEWING

• ½in/1.3cm seam allowance has been used throughout

Tent casing

1 With right sides together, stitch the striped fabric widths together along one long edge. Press the seams open and trim the selvages.

2 Repeat with the berry lining.

3 Place the two pieces right sides together. Align all raw edges. Pin to hold. Sew the two pieces together along the edges which will form the top of the wardrobe and the two sides only. Press. Turn right side out.

4 To the top edge of the berry lining, stitch a length of the loop side of the Velcro—this will be used to attach the fabric to the frame.

5 Stitch the hook side of Velcro to the same point on the striped outer fabric. The Vilene on the canopy will attach to this.

6 Using glue, and beginning at the back of the frame, stick the hook side of Velcro around the depth of the top shelf and the shelving unit at the corners.

7 Trim away the excess. Allow to dry. Discard the other remaining loop side of this length of Velcro.

8 Fit the fabric tent to the frame, aligning the loop side of the Velcro on the berry fabric with the hook side of the Velcro on the frame.

9 Begin 6in/15.2cm from the left-hand corner at the front of the frame and work around the back of the frame to the other side of the front.

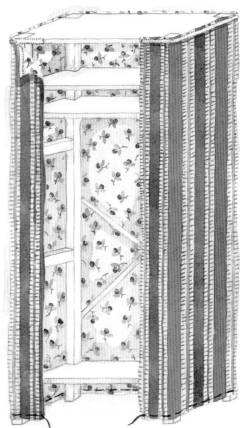

10 The length should clear floor level at this stage. Mark and remove the casing from the frame and trim the length accordingly.

11 Sew a line of permanent basting through both layers in the seam allowance at the bottom raw edges.

Binding

1 To prepare the binding for the bottom of the wardrobe, fold each binding strip in half lengthways, wrong sides together and press.

2 Open out the fold. Turn in ½in/1.3cm seam allowance to the center fold on each long edge and press. Open out the folds.

3 With right sides together align one short raw edge of one 7in/17.8cm length with that of a piece for the depth of the frame. Stitch the two together up to the pressed center foldline only, using ½in/1.3cm seam.

4 Leave a gap of 1½in/3.8cm, then sew the remaining ½in/1.3cm seam.

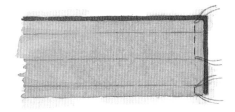

5 In the same way add the binding for the back of the wardrobe, then a second strip for the depth, then the remaining 7in/17.8cm length. Press the seams open.

6 Turn in the two short raw edges at the ends and stitch.

7 To stitch the binding to the striped side of the wardrobe, mark a line 2in/5cm above the raw edges of the striped fabric.

8 Align the first fold of the binding with the marked line, right sides together and stitched half uppermost. Pin and stitch together on the first foldline. *(see drawing top of next column)*

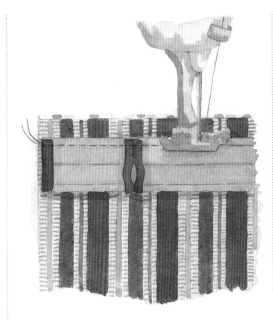

9 Refold the binding back over the stitching line so that the center foldline is at the bottom of the tent encasing the raw edges of the striped and berry fabrics. Turn in the seam at the remaining raw edge and pin to the berry fabric, so that the folded edge covers the previous stitching line. Baste in place.

10 To sew the remaining long edge of the binding in place, turn to the striped side of the wardrobe. Stitch along the seam line of the red binding and striped fabric, this will catch in the binding at the berry fabric side.

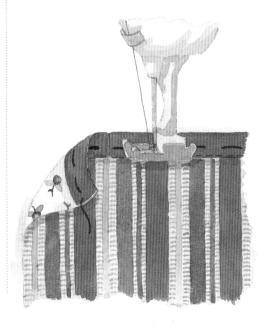

11 Remove the basting. Topstitch the short ends of the binding to the striped and berry fabrics.

12 The plastic weights are slotted into the holes remaining in the binding. Hand stitch the binding to hold the weights in place. Attach the wardrobe to the frame.

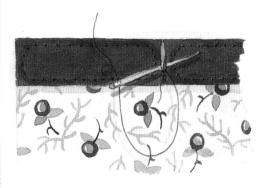

Shelf

1 To cover the bottom shelf, turn in ½in/1.3cm on all raw edges and press. Trim the corners.

2 Clip the diagonal at each corner and turn in a small seam allowance. Machine stitch the miters in place.

3 Turn in another ½in/1.3cm on the edge which will sit just above ground level and machine stitch in place.

4 Staple the fabric to the thickness of the shelf within the ½in/1.3cm seam allowance, pulling the fabric taut as you work.

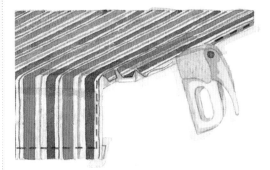

5 See step 9 Canopy on page 117 to calculate the quantity of braid.

Canopy

1 With right sides together and raw edges aligned, join the fabric widths.

2 At the outer ends, which will wrap around at the back of the canopy, turn in ½in/1.3cm and press. Turn in another ½in/1.3cm and stitch in place.

3 Pin one side of a length of Velcro to the seam allowance 8in/20.3cm above the raw edge which will form the scallop of the canopy.

4 Stitch the remaining half of Velcro to the seam allowance on the other side, so that the two pieces align.

5 To make the scalloped edge of the canopy, align one long edge of pelmet Vilene with the wrong side of the lower edge of the striped fabric and fuse the two together following the manufacturer's instructions. Because the two fabrics are bonded together, there is no seam allowance along this edge. Trim the short ends.

6 To form the scallop, using the pattern provided, trace the shape onto the bottom edge of the Vilene, centering the scallop along the width of the fabric. Cut out the shape using sharp scissors.

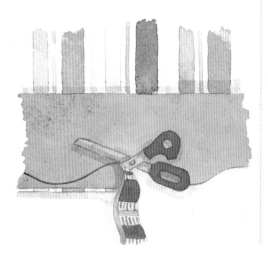

7 To calculate the amount of braid needed, measure the scalloped edge and add 1in/2.5cm to each end for turnings.

8 Pin and machine stitch the braid in place along the scallop, beginning at the center point and working outward to each side. Turn in the raw edge at each end.

9 Braid is also used to decorate the edges of the shelves. Add the length of three shelves to your calculation, (one is covered with fabric).

10 Glue the braid across the front edge of each shelf.

11 To form the gathered top edge of the canopy, at the remaining raw edge work two rows of long gathering stitches ½in/1.3cm from the raw edge using strong polyester thread.

12 Gather up the stitches tightly and stitch to hold. Stitch 18in/45.7cm ties to each side.

Assembling the canopy

1 When assembling the canopy, the scalloped edge sits 7½in/19cm below the top of the frame. It is held in place by the loop side of the Vilene which is bonded to the striped fabric sticking to the hook side of the Velcro at the top of the frame.

2 Starting at the center back align the top edge of the Vilene on the wrong side of the canopy with the strip of Velcro running around the top of the frame and tent casing.

3 As you return to the beginning, overlap the two edges and stick together with Velcro.

4 The ties are threaded down the cardboard tube and out at the opposite end. Give a sharp tug to pull the gathered up raw edges of the canopy down just inside the tubing to hide the edges.

5 Slide the cardboard tube over the length of the dowel and knot the ties tightly at the bottom of the dowel.

6 To the top of the dowel attach the painted finial.

Drapes

1 To make the drapes, turn in ¼in/6mm along each raw edge. Press.

2 Turn in another ¼in/6mm at each side. Press and machine stitch to hold.

3 At the bottom of the drape, turn in another seam allowance' width. Press with a damp cloth.

4 Wrap the weights in scraps of fabric. Stitch the wrapper to hold the weights securely.

5 Sew the hemline in place and stitch the weights in position.

6 Check the drape for length and adjust as necessary.

7 To make the casing to carry the wire at the top of the drape, turn in another ½in/1.3cm and sew. Press.

8 Thread the wire through the casing of each drape and attach to metal eyelets at each side of the wardrobe frame.

9 The wire should pass over the hook in the center front of the top shelf, which forms the roof of the tent.

Ianthe Screen

MATERIALS

Read the instructions before buying any fabric. The instructions given are for covering the frame design pictured right.

- Ianthe print for the screen
- Red for scallop and appliqué
- Braid
- Velcro
- Glue to attach the Velcro

MEASURING AND CUTTING

1 Yardage for each unit of the screen —Beginning at the bottom rung, measure up the frame, over the top rung and back to the beginning. Add 4in/10.2cm for turnings. Measure the width of one rung to determine the fabric width. Add 1in/2.5cm for turnings. Cut panels the length and width of your measurements.

2 The red scallop drops 7¼in/18.4cm at its lowest point at the back and front. Add 14½in/36.8cm + the thickness of the rung that the fabric passes over + 1in/2.5cm for seams. The fabric width is the width of the rung + 1in/2.5cm for turnings. Cut the required number.

3 Enlarge the scallop. Place the pattern at each end of the red. Draw around the shape and cut out.

4 For the red appliqué at the base of each unit, cut two pieces 3½in/8.9cm

long x the width of the rung + 1in/2.5cm for turnings.

5 Braid—Measure the scallop and add 1in/2.5cm for turnings.

6 Velcro—The bottom of each panel, = width of the rung. The fabric is also attached to each rung at the back and front with a small tab of Velcro. For each rung, not including the bottom one, allow 4in/10.2cm. Add this to your measurement. Cut each 4in/10.2cm strip into four squares.

SEWING

1 Panel—Turn in ¼in/6mm along each edge. Repeat, press and sew.

2 Scallop—Turn in ½in/1.3cm seam along each edge. Press.

3 Find the center on the long sides of each panel and match to the center on the straight sides of the scallop. Pin. Topstitch close to the edge of the red.

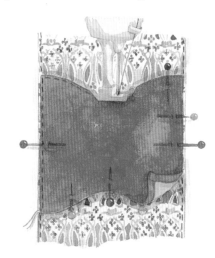

4 Pin the braid around the scallop. Turn in the raw edges. Sew in place.

5 To add the appliqué to the panel bottom, turn in ½in/1.3cm on one short and two long edges only. Press. Pin to the panel. Topstitch in place.

6 Place the loop half of the Velcro over the raw edge of the red. Sew in place. Sew the hook side to the other end of the panel. On the wrong side of each panel, mark the position of the rungs. Stitch the loop half of the tab to each side of the fabric to correspond with a rung. Glue the hook side to the rung.

~ Pinboard for the Dressing Room ~

When I was working on the dressing room my main preoccupation was one of storage. A system that was practical as well as pleasing to the eye—not something to be stowed away in a dark corner.

Fabric bags and fabric covered boxes of all shapes and sizes seemed a perfect solution. The bags can be hung off pegs in neat rows and the boxes carefully stacked.

The bag designs have been inspired by 1930s sewing bags, and beach bags. They can be decorated or left plain or made up of scrap fabrics—the possibilities are limitless. Use the designs opposite as a departure and make up your own fabric confections.

1 Stripe from the *Napier* collection

2 Tana lawn *(Capel)*

3 Geometric all-over sun-ray motif from the *Napier* collection

4 Trailing flower motif on a textured ground from the *Napier* collection

5 All-over lozenge design from the *Napier* collection

6 Manipulated fabric

7 Tana lawn *(Sophine)*

8 Tana lawn *(Madox)*

9 Tana lawn *(Bourton)*

10 Tana Lawn *(Meadow)*

11 Utrecht velvet

12 Tapestry braid

13 Decorative trims

14 Tassels

Patchwork Sewing Bag

Finished size 16¼in/41.3cm high

MATERIALS

- Red floral for the base and sides ~ 12in/30cm
- Four contrasting fabrics each ⅛yd/10cm wide, cut across the width of the fabric for the side panels
- Thick cord for the handle ~ 1yd/1m
- One large wooden bead
- Muslin for lining ~ ½yd/50cm

CUTTING

1 On cardboard draw a circle 9½in/24.1cm for the base of the bag. Cut out the shape and place it on the wrong side of the red floral fabric.

2 Draw around the outline using a fabric marker and cut out. Cut the same from muslin for the lining.

3 From the red floral and each of the four contrasting fabrics, for the bag sides, cut two lengths 21 x 3½in/53 x 9cm—ten in total.

4 From muslin for the side lining, cut one piece 14 x 30in/35.6 x 76.2cm. To bind the seams in the inside base of the bag, cut one strip 2 x 30in/5 x 76.2cm on the 45° bias.

SEWING

- ½in/1.3cm seams have been used throughout.

1 At one short end of each panel, turn down 4½in/11.5cm to the right side, for the decorative flap. Press.

2 Stitch down 2½in/6.4cm at each side of the fold.

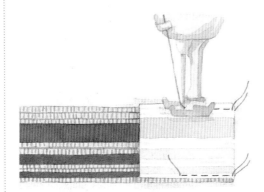

3 Pin the remaining 2in/5cm up toward the fold so that it does not get caught in the next stage of stitching.

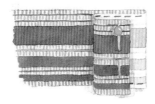

4 Place two panels right sides together with raw edges and folded edges aligned. Pin.

5 Stitch along one long edge from the point where the stitching for the flap commences and without catching in the pinned end of the flap. Press the seams open. *(see drawing, column 3)*

6 Repeat adding each panel in turn.

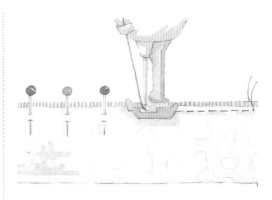

7 Fold the panels right sides together, aligning raw edges, and matching the ends of the decorative flaps. Baste the two edges together.

8 Starting at the flap edge, stitch ½in/1.3cm, leave a gap of 1in/2.5cm and continue to stitch to the bottom. The gap will eventually have cord threaded through for the handle.

9 Remove the pins from the loose end of the flaps. Turn the stitched and folded flaps out of the way. Pin and stitch together the 2in/5cm edges.

10 Turn the decorative flaps right side out and press.

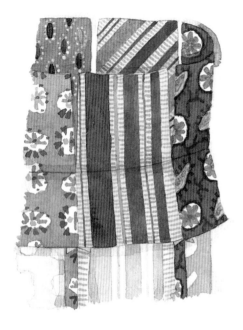

Lining

1 With right sides together, baste the two short ends of the muslin rectangle together. Try the lining for fit over the inside-out bag tube. Remove from the bag. Adjust the seam allowance as necessary and sew. Press the seam out.

2 Fold the decorative flap inside so that the 2½in/6.4cm edge stitched in step 2 Sewing stands proud of the bag.

3 Fit the lining to the bag, right sides together.

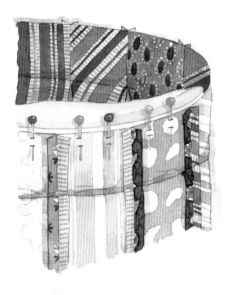

4 Aligning the muslin raw edge with the raw edge of the decorative flap. Pin and stitch together.

5 Turn right side out and push the lining inside the bag. Press.

6 Trim the excess lining away from the bottom of the bag.

7 Baste the lining to the sides within the seam allowance at the bottom.

Base

1 With wrong sides together, baste the circular lining to the red floral base within the seam allowance.

2 Turn the tube for the bag sides inside out and fit the base to the sides, pinning at regular intervals. Stitch in position and remove all basting.

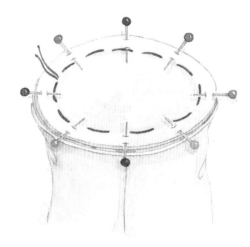

Finishing

1 To make the binding to cover the inside raw edges, fold the bias strip in half lengthways and press. Open out the fold.

2 Turn in the raw edges to the pressed center line and press.

3 Refold on the center line and press again. Open out all the folds.

4 Turn in one short end and press.

5 Align one long edge of binding with the raw edge at the base of the inner sides of the bag. Pin and machine stitch in position on the first fold. Begin stitching at the folded in short end.

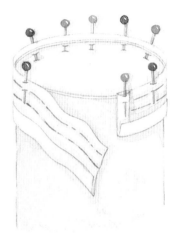

6 The remaining free tail end overlaps the start of the binding by 1½in/3.8cm. Trim the excess.

7 Fold the binding over to the base encasing raw edges in the binding. Slipstitch the remaining folded edge in position.

8 For the channel to thread the cord handle through, baste two lines around the bag on the right side of the fabric, just clearing the top and bottom of the 1in/2.5cm gap in the side seam.

9 Machine stitch along the basting lines, reinforcing the stitching close to the gap.

10 Insert the cord in the channel. Thread a bead over both ends of the cord and knot to secure. Unravel the cord ends to finish.

Manipulated Fabric Bag

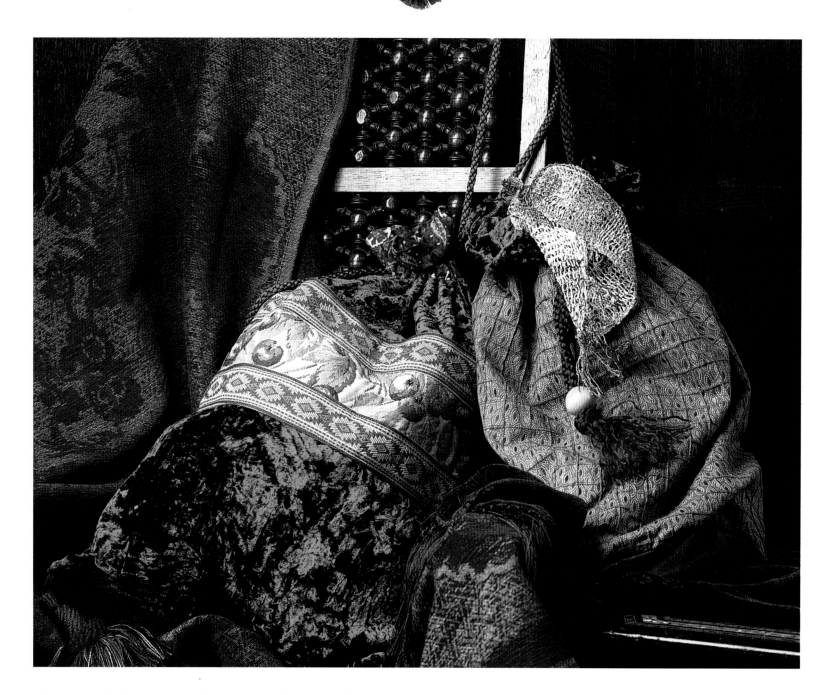

Finished size 19 x 7½in/
48.2 x 19.1cm diameter

MATERIALS

- Green print for the bag ~
  ½yd/50cm

- Red for the base ~ ¼yd/25cm
  square
- Green crushed velvet for
  the frill ~ 10 x 28in/25 x 71cm
- Lining ~ ½yd/50cm
- Red cord for the handle ~
  1yd/1m

- Two large wooden beads to
  thread the cord through
- Contrast sewing thread for
  the manipulated stitching
- 1in/2.5cm wide bias binding ~
  1yd/1m

PREPARATION—MAKING THE TEXTURED FABRIC

1 Wash and press the fabric. With a pencil and a ruler accurately draw a grid of ¾in/2cm squares on the right side of the green pattern fabric.

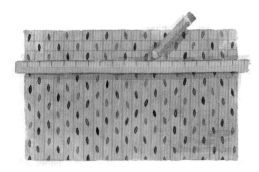

2 Insert twin needles following your sewing machine user's manual.

3 Thread the machine with a contrast color sewing cotton and set the machine stitch length to 9–12 stitches per inch/2–3mm.

4 Align the twin needles so that each stitches to each side of the drawn line. Following the marked grid, stitch a horizontal and vertical grid across the entire fabric. *(see fig 1 below)*

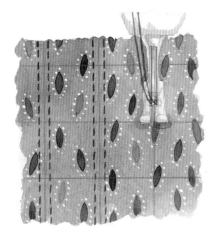

fig 1

5 If using a single needle, sew the two lines of stitching ⅛in/3mm apart, working lines of stitching in the same direction. *(see fig 2)*

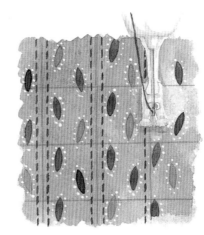

fig 2

CUTTING

1 From the manipulated fabric, cut one piece 16 x 27in/40.6 x 68.6cm.

2 For the base, on the wrong side of the fabric draw a circle 8in/20.3cm, and cut out.

3 From the bag lining, cut one piece 16 x 27in/40.6 x 68.6cm. For the base, cut one circle 8in/20.3cm.

4 For the trim, cut two pieces 9½ x 14in/24.1 x 35.6cm.

SEWING

• Use ½in/1.3cm seams throughout.

1 Place the velvet pieces right sides together. Pin along one short edge.

2 Measure and mark a point ½in/1.3cm from one end. Mark a second 1½in/3.8cm from the first.

3 Stitch at each side of the markers, leaving a 1½in/3.8cm gap through

which the cord for the handle will be threaded. Measure and mark the same points along the remaining short edges, but do not stitch at this stage.

4 Center the velvet frill along one long edge of the manipulated fabric right sides together and have the 1½in/3.8cm gap in the velvet toward the top. Pin and stitch in place. Press.

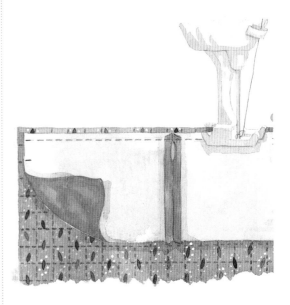

5 To the opposite long edge of velvet, align one long edge of the lining. Pin, stitch and press.

6 With right sides together, fold the panel in half widthways ensuring all seams are aligned. Pin and stitch leaving the 1½in/3.8cm gap (marked in step 2) in the green velvet.

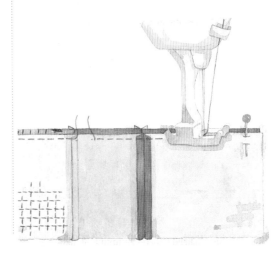

7 To make the channel to thread the cord handle through, turn the tube right side out. Fold the lining end down to the inside of the tube, turning with it 4⅛in/11.5cm of velvet. Pin the folded edge of velvet, then pin the raw edges of the tube.

8 Sew along the seam joining the bag sides to the trim and 1½in/3.8cm above it, aligning the stitching with the top of the gap in the velvet. Trim the excess lining level with the raw edges of the manipulated green. Turn the tube inside out.

9 Place the lining circle and the base wrong sides together and baste. With right sides together, accurately fit the base to the tube, aligning raw edges and pinning to hold.

10 Stitch the two together, reinforcing stitching as necessary. See illustration as for Patchwork Sewing Bag (step 2) on page 124. Grade the four raw edges to reduce bulk.

11 Bind the raw edges following the instructions for the Patchwork Sewing Bag on page 124.

12 Add the cord and wooden beads following the instructions for the Crushed Velvet Bag on page 129.

Above: *Four colorways of the Peacock Feather or Hera print, first designed by Arthur Silver for Liberty. This design was so universally popular that it became recognized as Liberty's trademark print. This classic design in soft, muted colors would be an ideal fabric choice for any of the bags featured in the Dressing Room.*

Crushed Velvet Bag

Finished size 20 x 13½in
50.8 x 34.3cm

MATERIALS

- Green crushed velvet ~
  ½yd/50cm
- Braid to decorate ~ 1yd/1m
- Red floral fabric for the trim ~
  ¼yd/25cm
- Lining ~ ½yd/50cm
- Cord for handle ~ 1yd/1m
- Two large wooden beads to fit
  over the double-width of cord
- Two tassels held on a braid

CUTTING

1 From velvet, cut one piece 18 x
28in/45.7 x 71.1cm.

2 From the red floral for the trim, cut
two pieces 10 x 14½in/25.4 x 36.8cm.

3 From lining, cut one piece 15½ x
28in/39.4 x 71.1cm.

4 Cut the length of cord for the
handle into two equal lengths.

SEWING

- Use ½in/1.3cm seam throughout.

1 If the selvages of the braid are
unfinished turn in the raw edges along
the length at each side and press.

2 Spread out the green velvet, right
side up on a clean flat surface. Across
the length of the fabric, 4½in/11.5cm

from the top edge position the braid. Pin in place and stitch along both sides.
Trim the braid to the width of the velvet.

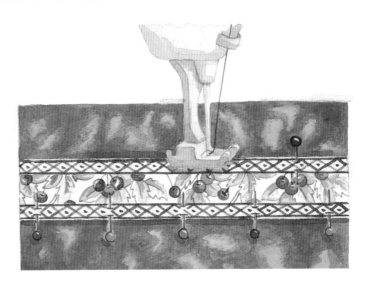

3 On one piece of red measure ½in/1.3cm from the corner along each
10in/25.4cm edge and mark with colored thread. Along the same edge mark a
second point 1in/2.5cm from the first. *(see illustration step 2 page 126)*

4 Place the two pieces right sides together. Align markers. Stitch above and below
the marked points at one side only. Press the seam open. The 1in/2.5cm gap is the
point where the handle is threaded through.

5 Place the red floral fabric and the
velvet right sides together. Have the
1in/2.5cm gap in the red floral at the
top and the pattern on the braid right
way up. Pin, baste and stitch the
pieces together. *(see fig 1)* Press the
seam toward the
green velvet.

6 With right sides
together, pin and
stitch the lining to
the top of the red
floral print. Press the
seam open.

fig 1

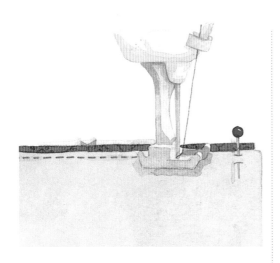

11 Pin and stitch down the length of the bag, starting and stopping at each side of the 1in/2.5cm gap, and keeping the tassels away from the stitching. Turn the bag right side out.

12 At the remaining raw edge of the lining, turn in ½in/1.3cm to the wrong side and press. On the right side of the fabric sew the two pieces together as close to the folded edge as possible. Push the lining into the bag so that the pressed foldline across the red fabric is at the top edge of the bag.

7 On the red floral, measure and mark a point 3¼in/8.3cm from the seam adjoining the green velvet. Fold the fabric on the marked line, wrong sides together and press with a damp cloth. The pressed fold is the bag top.

8 Trim the lining to the same length as the green velvet. Open out the fold.

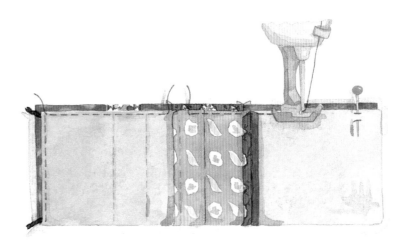

9 Right sides together, fold the fabric in half aligning the ends of the decorative braid and all seams. Press.

13 To define the channel through which the cord handle is threaded, stitch around the top edge of the green velvet through both layers of fabric. Accurately stitch a second line 1in/2.5cm away, aligning the stitching to clear the gap in the side seams. Baste the lines first if you need a guide.

10 At the bottom of the bag, baste the braid of one tassel in position at the marked fold and the second tassel at the corner of the green velvet. Pin and stitch across the short end of the green velvet and the braids holding the tassels at each end to form the bottom of the bag.

14 To define the bag bottom, turn the bag so that the tassel is toward the top and the side seam is facing you. Hold each side of the bag including the lining and pull down and out to make a triangle shape at the side seam.

15 Measure 1½in/3.8cm from this point and stitch a horizontal line across the marked point, stitching through the velvet and lining.

16 Repeat at the other side.

17 To add the handle, thread one length of cord through the channel in one side of the red floral fabric. Use a bodkin or a large eye needle.

18 Repeat at the other side of the bag with the second cord.

19 Thread a large wooden bead over the ends of both cords at both sides.

20 Knot the cords to hold the beads in place. Fray the ends of the strands.

Pinwheel Bag

prints, cut two strips 3in/7.6cm wide across the width of the fabric.

3 For the gusset, cut two strips 3 x 30in/7.6 x 76.2cm. Place right sides together aligning short ends. Stitch to make a strip 3 x 59in/7.6 x 149.9cm. Cut and piece the same from lining.

4 From lining, cut two circles 16in/40.6cm diameter.

5 From scraps, cover two buttons.

SEWING

• Use ½in/1.3cm seam throughout.

1 Place two wedges right sides together. Stitch along one straight edge. Repeat, adding a third wedge. Press seams open. Repeat.

2 Pin two halves right sides together. Align center points. Stitch from the center to the outer edge.

3 Rejoin at the center, then sew to the opposite side. Trim. Press.

Finished size 15in/38.1cm diameter x 2in/5cm deep

MATERIALS

• Five different fabrics for the wedge shapes, four of which should be 8 x 16in/20 x 41cm; and one to be 16 x 16in/41 x 41cm
• Green print for the gusset of the bag ~ 6 x 30in/16 x 77cm
• Three different print fabrics for the handles each 6in x 1yd/

16cm x 1m
• Lining ~ ¾yd/70cm
• Two self-cover buttons
• Zipper ~ 16in/40cm

CUTTING

1 Use the template on page 142 and cut twelve wedge shapes for the bag front and back. Cut two from each of four fabrics and four from one fabric. Divide into two groups of six wedges.

2 For the handles, from each of three

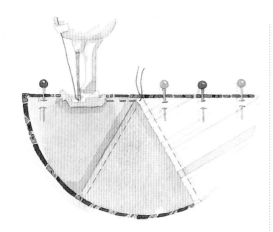

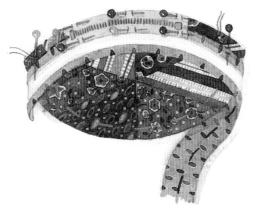

4 Baste a lining circle to the wrong side of each pieced circle. Treating the fabrics as one piece, turn in ½in/1.3cm around the raw edges. Press. In the seam, mark the zipper position on the right side of one circle.

5 Place the lining and gusset wrong sides together. Baste. Turn in ½in/1.3cm on all sides. Press.

6 Start at the bottom center of the bag back. Place the gusset right sides together and ease halfway around the circle, over the zip position. Pin. Sew 2in/5cm only at each side of the zip position, to ease handling.

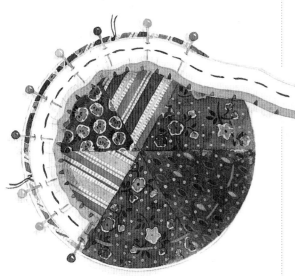

7 Baste the opening for the zip. On the lining side, place the zip right side down, centring it between the seamline of the back and gusset. Baste.

8 Check the zip opening. Sew both sides of the zip. Remove the basting.

9 Continue to pin the gusset in place. Mark the point of overlap and trim to ½in/1.3cm longer.

10 Undo the pins at the start and end of the gusset. Sew across the short ends. Pin in place. Put to one side.

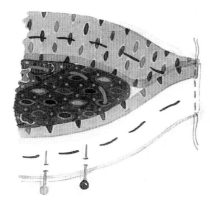

11 To make the handles, fold each strip in half lengthways. Press. Draw a diagonal at one short end.

12 Sew the diagonal and along the long raw edges, leaving the remaining short end free.

13 Reduce the bulk of the raw edges at the seam. Turn right side out. Press.

14 Stack three strips, aligning raw edges. Sew together. Plait the lengths and pin to hold. Repeat for the other

handle. Place the handle between the bag and gusset, 2in/5cm above the zip. Stitch in place in the seam allowance.

15 Stitch the circle to the gusset, carefully easing the fabric in around the curves and catching in the raw edges of the handle.

16 Open the zip a fraction to ensure the bag can be turned right side out when constructed.

17 Fit the front to the gusset, and pin in place. Position the other side of the handle opposite the first. Baste and sew in the seam allowance.

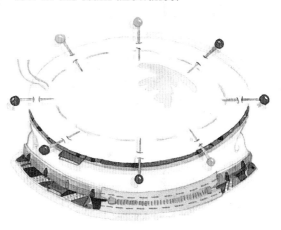

18 Stitch the front in place. Turn the bag right side out to check the fit. Turn inside out. Machine overcast the raw edges.

19 The handles are held together with a tab. From a fabric scrap, cut one tab 2½ x 1in/6.4 x 2.5cm. Turn in ¼in/6mm all around and press.

20 Wrap the tab around the plaits approximately 4in/10.2cm from the tail ends and stab stitch in place to hold the handles secure.

21 Add a fabric covered button to the center of the bag front and back.

Covered Hat Boxes

MATERIALS

- **A purchased cardboard hat box**
- **Fabric A ~ lid, rim, inside lid**
- **Fabric B ~ sides, base, box inner**
- **Braid to trim the lid, cord for the handle, metal eyelets, cardboard, double-sided tape**

DETERMINING QUANTITIES

1 Fabric A—Lid and rim (inside and out) = rim measurement x 4, + lid diameter + 4in/10.2cm. Inside lid = diameter of lid + 2in/5cm.

2 Fabric B—Sides = box circumference + 2in/5cm. Width of the strip = box depth + 2in/5cm. Estimate the same for the box inner. Base = diameter + 2in/5cm. Estimate the same for the box inner base.

3 Braid = Circumference of the rim. Handle = Twice the rim diameter.

4 Box inner—From cardboard cut one piece the circumference of the box. Cut the width ¼in/6mm less than the height of the box without the lid. Fit inside the box and trim to fit.

5 Inside base, lid lining, outside base—Cut a cardboard circle to fit. Cut all fabrics.

MAKING

1 Lid and rim—Fix strips of adhesive across the top and around the circumference of the rim, inside and out. Remove the tape backing from the lid and outside rim. Press the fabric for the box lid. Place right side down. Center the lid right side down on top. Pull the fabric taut across the surface, without distorting the pattern. Ease the fabric over the rim and inside the rim making small pleats. Remove the tape backing. Press the fabric into place. Trim to fit.

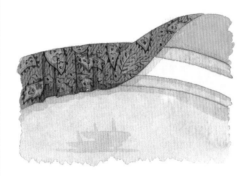

2 Apply adhesive to the cardboard circle on one side only. Remove the backing. Stretch a pressed square of fabric over the circle, smoothing out the fabric with the palm of your hand. Trim the excess leaving 1in/2.5cm to fold to the wrong side. Apply tape to the other side of the circle. Remove the backing. Pleat the fabric onto the tape. Stick the lid liner in position.

3 Sides—At one short end of the fabric strip, turn in a 1in/2.5cm seam. Press. Stick in place. Apply tape to the fabric seam and remove the backing. Apply tape to the top and bottom circumference of the box. Remove the backing. Beginning at the back, wrap the fabric around the box, leaving excess fabric at upper and lower edges. Pull the fabric taut. As you reach the beginning, turn in the raw edge to make a neat join.

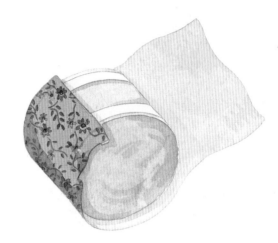

4 Apply tape to the top inner side of the box and box base. Pleat the fabric into place at both ends.

5 Base, inside and out—See step 2.

6 Inside liner—Apply tape to both sides of the cardboard. Stretch the fabric across the cardboard and smooth in place. Adhere the liner to the box.

7 Make small holes for the eyelets. Thread the cord through the eyelets. Knot the ends. Glue braid to the rim.

Techniques and Templates

FABRIC PREPARATION

Before buying fabrics ensure that they are suitable for the intended purpose and that if you need to adapt any instructions you buy the correct amount.

- Wash and iron all fabrics carefully to take care of shrinkage.
- Remove the selvages.
- Before cutting make sure the fabric pieces are straight and that you are cutting on a straight grain, unless the instructions state otherwise.
- Cut long lengths such as borders from the fabric first.
- Cut long lengths parallel to the selvages where there is sufficient fabric to allow it.

MAKING AND USING TEMPLATES

The templates are all drawn to the finished size so when cutting the fabrics add the required seam allowance all around each shape, except where the chosen method of appliqué is using fusible web.

1 Make the templates in template plastic or cardboard to the full size. Transfer all the information onto the templates.

2 Carefully draw the templates onto tracing paper using a sharp pencil and a ruler to mark the straight lines.

3 Glue the tracing paper onto the cardboard, then cut out using a metal ruler and art knife for the straight lines

and scissors for the curves. If translucent template plastic is being used, trace the template outlines onto the plastic and cut out in the same way.

APPLIQUÉ

Appliqué literally means applying one fabric to another. The method was devised as a means to decorate or embellish a plain background fabric. Many methods of appliqué have evolved including Hawaiian, shadow and reverse appliqué. However, just two methods have been used in the projects in this book—conventional needle-turned hand appliqué and bonded appliqué using fusible web with machine satin stitch to protect the raw edges.

NEEDLE-TURNING METHOD

1 Place the template right side up on the right side of the fabric.

2 Lightly draw around the shape. Cut out adding by eye a scant ¼in/6mm margin all around for seams.

3 With finger and thumb pinch the turnings to the wrong side without stretching the fabric.

4 If required, with a sharp pair of scissors clip into the seam allowance at curves or sharp angles, up to but not breaching the drawn pencil line and at a 90° angle to it.

5 Pin and lightly baste the shapes if you are working with a complex

design. For single appliqué shapes pin each to the background and using the tip of your needle, stroke the seam allowance under and blindhem or slipstitch to the background. The aim is to apply the shape as invisibly as possible.

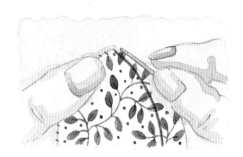

USING FUSIBLE WEB

Fusible web is an adhesive product which is applied to the reverse of one layer of fabric using the heat of an iron, in order to fuse it to a second layer of fabric beneath. It has one slightly rough side, the "web" and one smooth peel-away paper side. Fusible web provides a quick, easy and convenient method of permanently applying layers of fabric to each other. Once bonded in place the edges are stitched, simultaneously adding a decorative edge and hiding any uneven raw edges.

1 On the smooth side of fusible web trace or draw your chosen shape without seam allowances. Reverse the design where appropriate.

2 Using sharp scissors rough cut out the shape leaving a margin of at least ⅛in/3mm around the drawn line.

3 Place the chosen fabric right side down on the ironing board. On top place the shape, fusible web side down. Place baking parchment over the surface to protect the iron.

4 Following the manufacturer's instructions for the heat setting of the iron and the length of time it takes to bond the web to the fabric, fuse the two together. Allow to cool.

5 With sharp scissors cut out the exact shape on the drawn pencil line—the method ensures that the web is distributed to the edges of the fabric and will not peel once fused in its final position. Remove the paper backing to reveal the web.

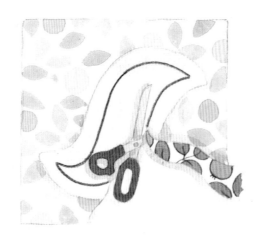

6 Place the fabric shape, web side down on the right side of the background fabric in the desired position. Place a layer of baking parchment over the top of the fabric and fuse the fabric shapes together following the manufacturer's instructions. Allow to cool.

7 Stitch in place using either machine satin stitch or buttonhole stitch, with the stitches set close together.

MACHINE SATIN STITCH
used for applying shapes with fusible web

If you are working with a variety of fabric types or are new to using a sewing machine, always work a test sample on representative fabric scraps before beginning work on the project. Satin stitch adds the finishing touch to the design, so it would be a shame to ruin a lot of hard work with inconsistent stitching and incorrect tension.

As a rule satin stitch is worked with the stitching very close together. For small motifs use a stitch width set at 12 stitches per inch/2mm, and for larger motifs use a stitch width of 6 stitches per inch/4mm. Set the stitch length using your manual as a guide—the longer the length the more open the stitch and the more the stitch will appear as a zigzag. Closely set stitches will appear as satin stitch.

APPLIQUÉ PERSE

Appliqué perse employs the same techniques as conventional appliqué, except here the shapes are cut from fabric pre-printed with defined shapes such as flowers. The technique developed as a means of extending the life of rare or precious fabrics. The shapes, once cut, are re-arranged on a background fabric to produce an entirely different design.

1 Cut the shapes out as for the needle-turning method above, adding the seam allowance to the outline of the motif. Once stitched in place the outline of the motif will form the edges of the shape.

2 Choose a thread of an appropriate color. If you choose a contrasting color, the shape will have a defined outer edge, particularly if the shape is

Buttonhole stitch

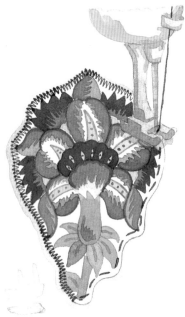

Machine satin stitch

Slipstitch

applied using buttonhole stitch or machine satin stitch. If you intend to use an invisible stitch, pick a neutral color thread which will allow the stitching to merge into the background and focus attention on the printed design.

CUSHIONS

Preparing the two halves of the cushion back for a centered zipper.

The instructions given are for working right-handed. If you are left-handed reverse all the instructions.

1 If desired overlock the raw edge of the turned in edges.

2 On each of the two pieces for the cushion back, turn 1in/2.5cm to the wrong side on one long edge only.

3 Place both pieces right sides together, open out the pressed edge and baste along the pressed line.

4 Stitch just 1in/2.5cm in from each end on the pressed line. Press the seams to the left-hand side.

INSERTING A ZIPPER

1 Place the zipper in the basted opening wrong side up and baste down the left-hand side only.

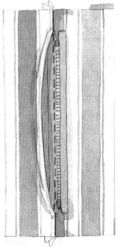

2 Flip the left-hand piece of the cushion over the right-hand piece, right sides together.

3 Turn the top seam allowance out of the way so that the

zipper is visible. Stitch in position using the pressed line as a guide and sewing to the left of the teeth. The stitching will penetrate a single layer of fabric. The zipper can be stitched by hand using back stitch.

4 Fold the back into the correct position. Turn the zipper so that the right side is facing upward and so that the free side of the zipper is concealed by the seam allowance of the left-hand side. This will turn the 1in/2.5cm seam to the right.

5 Baste the zipper to the left-hand half of the cushion back, ½in/1.3cm from the folded edge. Stitch in place and reinforce the stitching at each end of the zipper. Remove the basting.

MAKING UP A CUSHION

1 Open the zipper for a few inches/centimetres.

2 Place the cushion front and back right sides together. Match and pin the center points on each side, then the corners.

3 Baste and stitch through all the layers in the seam allowance. If piping has been added baste as close as possible to the cord.

4 Tie off the threads. Open the zipper fully and turn right side out. Press. Insert the cushion pad.

MITERING BORDERS

1 Press all fabric pieces.

2 With right sides together, center each border along each side of the project. Align raw edges. There should be a border's width' excess fabric overhanging at each side. Pin the borders to the project.

3 Stitch each border to the project without sewing into any seams.

4 At each corner overlap the borders.

5 Turn under the excess fabric of the top border piece back on itself, to make a fold with a 45° angle. The

turned under edge should be parallel with the border strip below.

6 Pin to hold and lightly press, removing the pins just before pressing.

7 Slipstitch the miter in position. Check that it lies flat before trimming the excess.

8 Trim the excess from the borders. Repeat at the remaining corners.

MAKING CONTINUOUS BINDING

Binding cut on the 45° bias has more stretch and elasticity in it than that cut on the straight grain, making it an ideal choice for binding curves.

1 To avoid a large number of seams begin with as large a rectangle of fabric as possible. Trim all edges straight to the grain and ensure that all corners are true right angles. Press.

2 To find the 45° bias, pick up one corner and fold it so that the raw edge on the shorter end of the rectangle aligns with the raw edge of one long end. Lightly crease the diagonal and cut along the creased line. Repeat at the opposite end.

3 If fabric is at a premium, stitch the cut off triangle to the opposite end.

4 On the wrong side of the fabric draw lines across the fabric parallel to the 45° bias raw edge. Consult the project instructions for details of the width of the binding.

5 On the straight top and bottom of the rectangle rule a line ¼in/6mm from the raw edge.

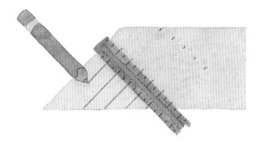

6 Mark point A on the fabric at the top left-hand corner. Mark point B at the bottom left-hand corner on the first drawn pencil line.

7 Fold the fabric in half so that right sides are facing and shift the fabric slightly so that points A and B meet.

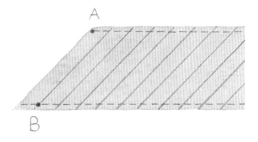

8 Hold the two points together with a pin.

9 Continue to insert pins perpendicular to the fabric at intervals along the raw edges, ensuring that all the drawn pencil lines correspond.

10 Stitch along the ¼in/6mm ruled line and carefully press the seam open. Begin at point A/B and carefully cut along the spiral pencil line.

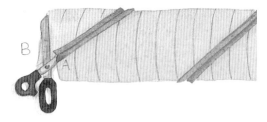

COVERING PIPING CORD

1 Boil the cotton piping cord to shrink it, allow to dry. Synthetic cords should not be boiled.

2 Make continuous binding or join together sufficient bias tape to the required length, remembering to add an extra allowance for turning corners and overlapping at the start and finish.

3 Fold the binding in half lengthways sandwiching the piping cord in the fold and baste. Using the zipper foot on the sewing machine or by hand, baste as close as possible to the cord, holding it within the binding.

ATTACHING PIPING

1 Beginning at the center of the bottom of the project, pin, then baste the piping to the right side of the project. Align the raw edges of the bias strips with those of the project.

2 To ease the piping around any right angles, clip the seam allowance three times at each corner without breaching the stitching line.

3 As you return to the beginning, unpick a little machine basting to allow the cord to be trimmed. Either trim the cord to the exact length so that the two ends meet each other, or

unravel the ends and twist the two cords together.

4 Trim the covering to 1in/2.5cm longer than the raw edge at the beginning. Turn in ¼in/6mm at one end and enclose the other end within it. Stitch in place close to the piping using a zipper foot.

MAKING A QUILT SANDWICH

1 Place the backing right side down on a clean, flat surface. Smooth out the wrinkles and tape down at approximately 6in/15.2cm intervals. This will keep the fabric flat while the sandwich is basted together.

2 Center the batting on the backing. Center the quilt top on the batting, right side up. Pin from the center out, smoothing the fabric out as you go.

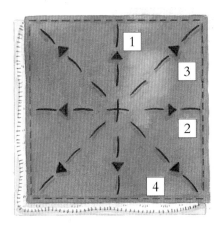

3 Baste the sandwich together following the sequence in the

diagram. Add extra rows of basting parallel to rows 1, 2, 3 and 4.

QUILTING

Quilting is the running stitch which holds the layers of a quilt or project together. It can be worked by hand or machine. Quilting adds interest and texture to a surface, or can be used to emphasize motifs within the project.

• The hand quilting stitch is a simple, straight running stitch which should be neat and even.

• Choose a quilting thread that is pre-waxed, so that the thread pulls smoothly and easily through the layers of the project without knotting.

• Pick a color that is neutral and blends with the background surface.

• Begin quilting in the center of the project and work outward. This allows the different fabrics and filling room to move against each other.

• Many quilters choose to use a wooden hoop for hand quilting large projects to help keep an even tension over the surface of the quilt.

• Quilting in-the-ditch refers to adding a line of stitching along or close to existing seam lines.

BINDING USING CONTINUOUS BINDING

1 True up the edge of the quilt and insert a line of permanent basting within the seam allowance.

2 Beginning 6in/15.2cm from one corner of the project, align the raw edges of the binding with the raw edges of the right side of the project. Pin the binding to the project.

3 As you reach the first corner, stop pinning a seam allowance' width from the corner. Sew the binding to the first side.

4 To create a miter, fold the binding away from the quilt at a 90° angle.

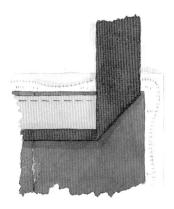

5 Hold the binding at the corner, then bring the binding down to run parallel with the next side. This movement will create a triangular pleat with sufficient fabric at the corner to make a miter.

6 Continue pinning along the next side. Stitch carefully down the second side until a seam allowance' width from the next corner.

7 Repeat at each corner.

8 As you return to the beginning, trim the binding at least 1in/2.5cm longer than needed.

9 Turn under ¼in/6mm seam allowance on the short end and overlap the two ends and sew in place.

10 Fold the binding over the raw edges of the project.

11 Turn in a seam allowance on the remaining long edge.

12 Pin in place so that the binding covers the line of stitching attaching the binding to the front.

13 Either slipstitch in place by hand *(see stitch glossary below)* or turn the project over to the front, baste the binding in place and machine stitch along the seam line joining the binding to the front.

STITCH GLOSSARY

Running Stitch

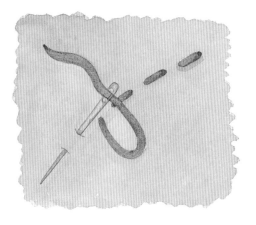

Ladder Stitch

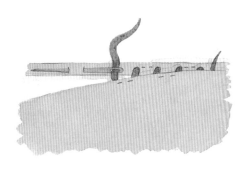

Blanket/Buttonhole Stitch

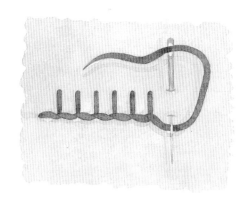

Whipped Back Stitch

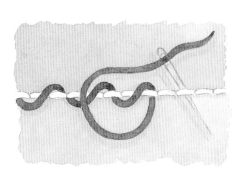

Blindhem Stitch

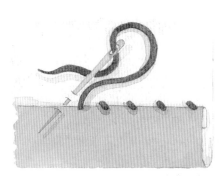

Slipstitch

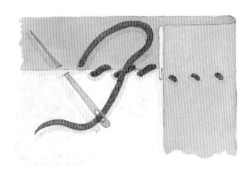

POTS OF LILIES CUSHION (ACTUAL SIZE)   BOLSTER CUSHION (ACTUAL SIZE)

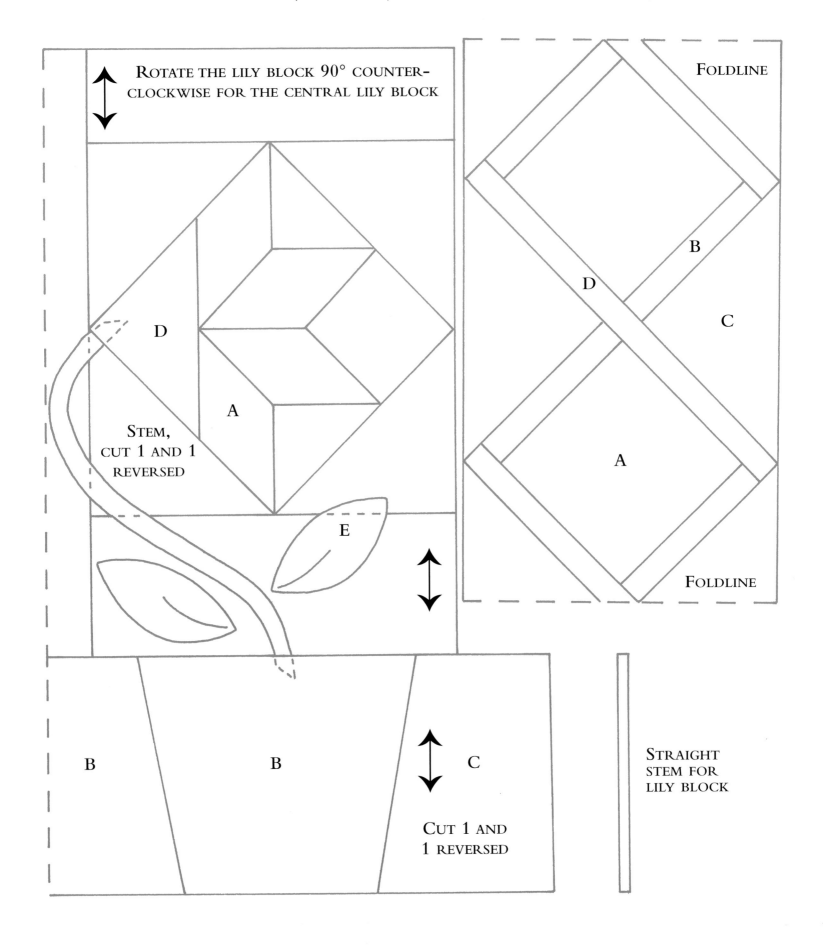

ROTATE THE LILY BLOCK 90° COUNTER-CLOCKWISE FOR THE CENTRAL LILY BLOCK

FOLDLINE

B

D

C

D

A

STEM,
CUT 1 AND 1
REVERSED

E

FOLDLINE

B   B   C

CUT 1 AND
1 REVERSED

STRAIGHT
STEM FOR
LILY BLOCK

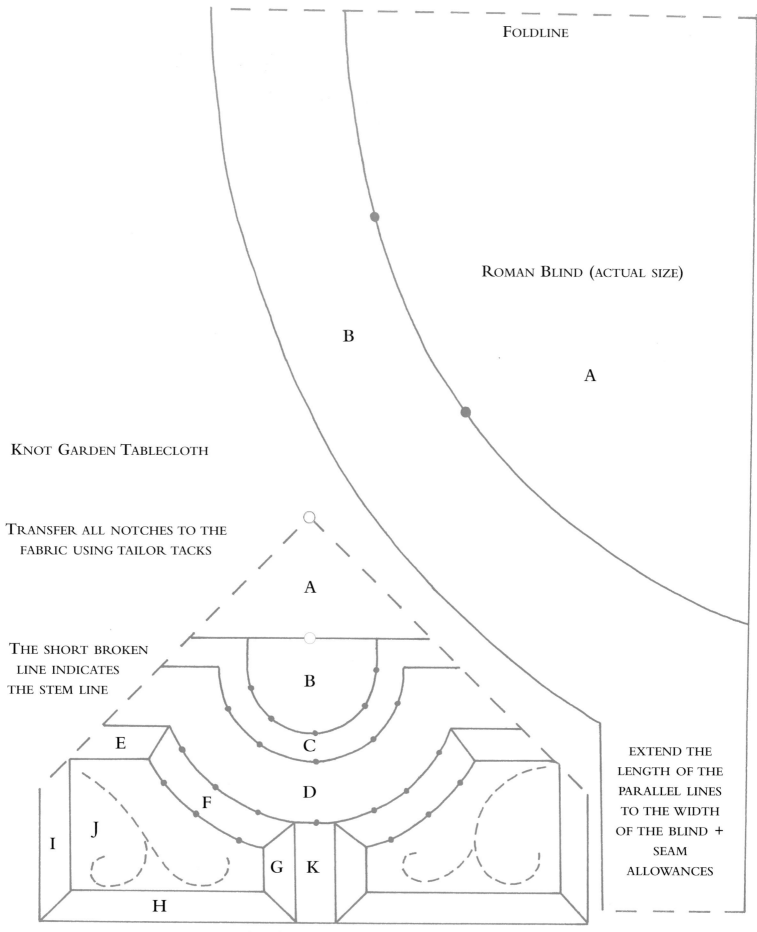

FOLDLINE

ROMAN BLIND (ACTUAL SIZE)

B

A

KNOT GARDEN TABLECLOTH

TRANSFER ALL NOTCHES TO THE
FABRIC USING TAILOR TACKS

A

THE SHORT BROKEN
LINE INDICATES
THE STEM LINE

B

C

E

F

D

EXTEND THE
LENGTH OF THE
PARALLEL LINES
TO THE WIDTH
OF THE BLIND +
SEAM
ALLOWANCES

I

J

G

K

H

ENLARGE TO 5¾IN/14.6CM BETWEEN THE DOTS

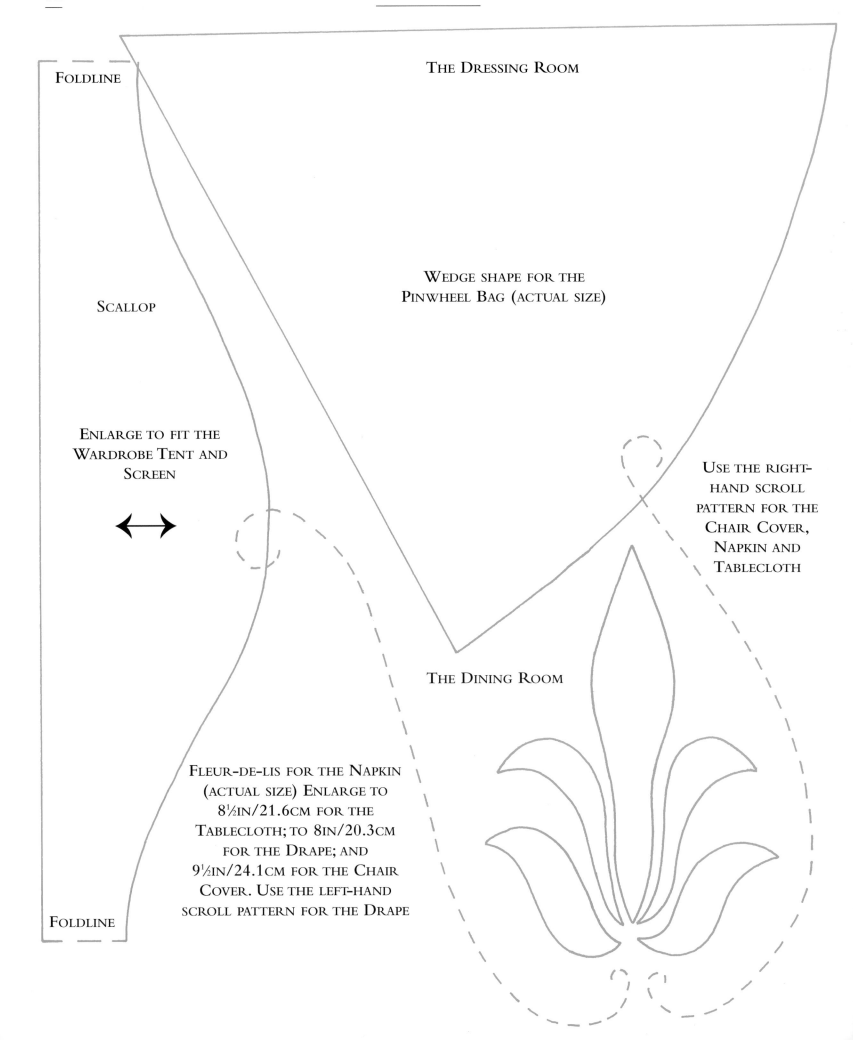

FOLDLINE

THE DRESSING ROOM

SCALLOP

WEDGE SHAPE FOR THE
PINWHEEL BAG (ACTUAL SIZE)

ENLARGE TO FIT THE
WARDROBE TENT AND
SCREEN

USE THE RIGHT-
HAND SCROLL
PATTERN FOR THE
CHAIR COVER,
NAPKIN AND
TABLECLOTH

THE DINING ROOM

FLEUR-DE-LIS FOR THE NAPKIN
(ACTUAL SIZE) ENLARGE TO
8½IN/21.6CM FOR THE
TABLECLOTH; TO 8IN/20.3CM
FOR THE DRAPE; AND
9½IN/24.1CM FOR THE CHAIR
COVER. USE THE LEFT-HAND
SCROLL PATTERN FOR THE DRAPE

FOLDLINE

The Nursery

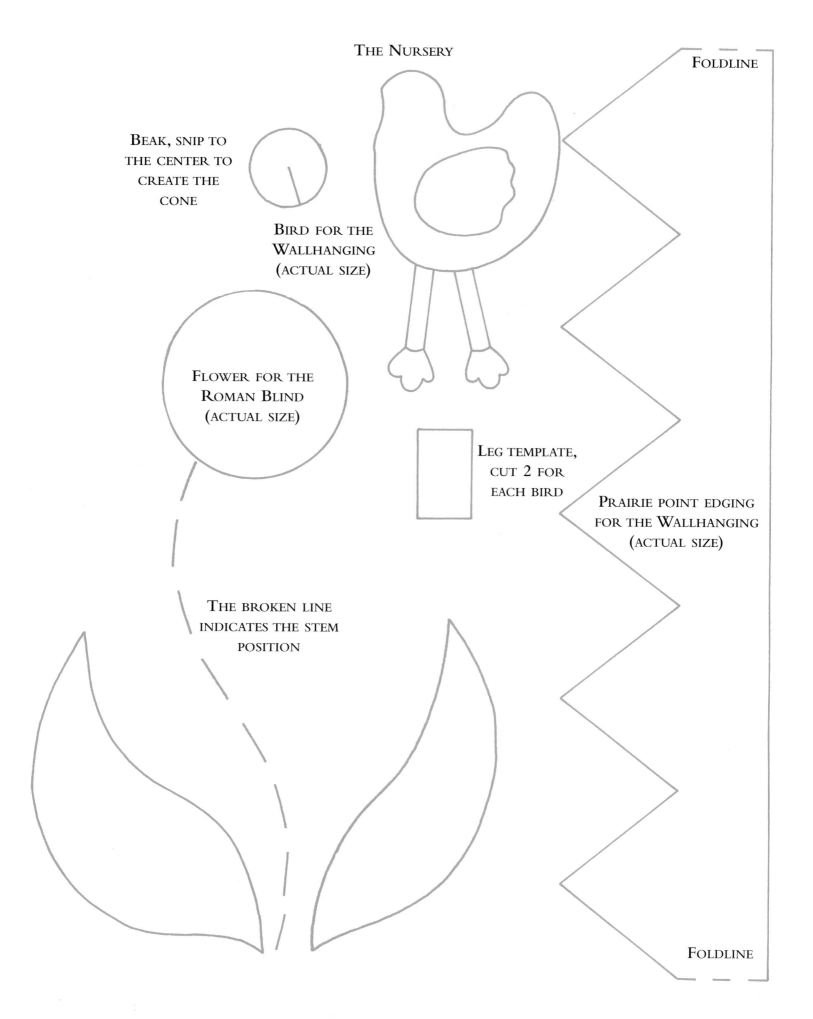

Beak, snip to the center to create the cone

Bird for the Wallhanging (actual size)

Flower for the Roman Blind (actual size)

Leg template, cut 2 for each bird

The broken line indicates the stem position

Foldline

Prairie point edging for the Wallhanging (actual size)

Foldline